# Ariana Sings
## One Woman's Journey to Find Her Voice

Rebecca E. Grant

Edited by Courtney Dowd

Thinking From the Heart
Publications

Thinking From the Heart Publications
A division of TFH™
Minnetonka, Minnesota
Website: www.thinkingfromtheheart.com


Published in the United States of America
by Thinking From the Heart Publications
a division of TFH™

ISBN: 978-0-578-05645-6

Printed in the United States of America
Set in Times New Roman

Cover Art: Watercolor: *Evening Sea Cliffs* by Tracy Griffin, Artist
GriffinArtStudios.com
tracy.griffin@hotmail.com

The words, intentions, hopes, dreams, images and truths of this story are dedicated to every living soul in the spirit of one love.

One day
one of those strangers would introduce
herself to me, and then
the life I'd never been able to foresee
would begin, and everything
before I became myself would appear
necessary to the rest of the story.

— Lawrance Raab from *My Life Before I Knew It*

# Introduction

The name **ARIANA** came to me in those softly descending moments before sleep. It was a breathy melody, full of light. A confection so whisper-sweet, I knew it was the voice of my spiritual guides revealing the true name of my soul. This is how they typically come to me, murmuring gently into my right ear in a language I do not understand, but which leaves me with many impressions that I know to be truth.

Most of the information in this story is not so much about learning something new as it is about remembering what we already know. Whether myth or truth, it is reported that for the nine months we are in the womb, Archangel Gabriel shares all the secrets of the universe we will need to know. Then, just before we are born, he silences us by placing his finger on our lips to ensure the safety of the divine secrets. The cleft below our nose is evidence that Gabriel has prepared us.

Upon being born, our humanness requires that we learn the ways of being human, including the gift of inhabiting a body that allows us simple pleasures like the feel of cool water on a hot day, the slow unraveling of muscles through the practice of Tai Chi, or the ability to smooth away errant hair from the forehead of a child. It is only after we learn to be human that we are free to begin remembering the divine secrets of Life and Light.

The story that follows is entirely about miracles; the miracle of love, light, truth, life, healing, joy, fulfillment and purpose. It is about how God is as much in us as around us.

Every human being is divinely unique. Only you can decide for yourself what to believe. My fervent hope is that the spiritual truths shared in this story will in some way contribute to the fulfillment of your purpose in this lifetime.

Joyful remembering!

*"...the heart has reasons that reason does not understand."*
— Jacques Benigne Bossuel

# *Beginnings*

I watched in horror—as if it were not happening to me—as if I were an amorphous entity observing from above. My car had skidded off the freeway and was sliding down the soft embankment.

It was spring of 1982 and I was driving to work in a car that had been my mother's six months earlier, until she died and left it to me. I was doing about 65 miles an hour balancing a lid-less mug of coffee with the steering wheel because in those days, neither drink holders nor Starbucks were as yet cultural norms. *Eye of the Tiger* by *Survivor* was playing. I was singing along and tapping the toe of my foot.

About five miles into my drive, the music began to distort and then stopped. I glanced at the dashboard and saw loops of brown magnetic tape spilling out of the cassette player. My first thought was to try to save the tape. I rolled down the window, dumped my coffee, tossed the mug into the back seat, and attempted a one-handed save.

How long was my attention diverted? Two seconds? Five? When I next looked, the car was sliding down the soft embankment.

Panicked thoughts spooled in my brain much like the cassette tape. Was I going to get hurt? How badly? Would I survive?

Too late to stop the momentum, I pulled my hands from the steering wheel and covered my face. But instead of tumbling out-of-control, I felt the car shift very suddenly and begin to right itself. I looked through my fingers and couldn't believe what I saw. My car was rolling effortlessly up the embankment and back onto the freeway, as if someone or something was driving for me.

ৡৡৡৡ

Is the future planned, or is it an array of possibilities?

What about miracles? Do you believe in them?

Have you ever asked for, or experienced a miracle?

How often have you heard someone exclaim, "Why, it's a *miracle!*" or "It *must* be a miracle!" or even "It will take a *miracle!*"

Miracles are on our minds whether we believe in them or not. When we don't know how to explain something, we often attribute it to a miracle. When we are desperate, disconsolate, and don't know where else to turn, we sometimes ask for a miracle. When we are burning with passion for something or someone but can't seem to make it happen, we sometimes try to bargain for a miracle.

We ask, even if we don't entirely believe in them.

And, when we are given a miracle, we often use logic to explain the miracle away. If logic doesn't work, we set explanation aside and say, "Who knows?"

Which is exactly what I did that spring day in 1982. By the time I got to work I had shrugged it off because I had no logical explanation.

Twenty years later in 2002 I invited my family and some friends over for Thanksgiving dinner. The turkey was roasting in the oven along with a carrot custard so creamy it could pass for dessert. A pan of potatoes and a pot of squash were simmering on the stove top, and a corn pudding was in the microwave on low. I ran a mental check and nodded. Things were nicely on schedule. This was the perfect time to pop into the bathroom.
The moment I closed the door, I heard it. The door handle clicked in a funny way and I just knew something had malfunctioned. Sure enough, the door handle slipped like a stripped screw and would not retract the latch. I was locked in a 4x4 windowless room. I had no phone, no tools; no visible means of getting myself out of that room. I wasn't expecting anyone for at least an hour and with all the food cooking, fire was my greatest concern, to say

nothing of the fact that I am not overly fond of small places.

My first reaction was to experience the incredulity of the situation. How does an adult get locked in the bathroom? Why did I even shut the door? I was alone in my apartment. I almost never shut the door when I'm alone!

Panic threatened.

I banged, pushed, lunged, lifted, all of which produced a lot of noise, but no freedom. Nothing I tried, worked. Finally I hunkered down on the toilet seat to calm myself. I could smell the squash starting to scorch. In my opinion, it takes a lot of putsy work to make a good squash. There's all that peeling and cutting and seeding. The thought of my squash burning was very grounding and I heard myself say, "I'm going to need a miracle here."

In that moment, I felt myself grow still. In fact, I felt everything around me grow still, which sounds a little strange, because it's not like there was anyone else with me in that bathroom. In those moments absent of even a whisper or whir, I was given the strong impression that if I tried the door handle again and believed it would open, it would in fact open.

I didn't hesitate. I leaped up and grasped the door handle forcefully. It slid as uselessly as before. For one sickening moment I thought how foolish I had been to believe I was somehow being divinely freed. I sat back down on the toilet seat and was once again given an impression that help was present, I had only to believe.

Alright, I thought. Let's try this. I am *not* trapped. I *asked* for help and I will *get* it!" I reached out and pulled gently on the door. It opened as if there had never been a problem.
Later that day several people looked at the door handle. Everyone agreed the handle was malfunctioning, and one of them removed it to avoid a reoccurrence. Yet, while everyone agreed the door handle was malfunctioning, each had a different opinion about how I managed to get out of the bathroom.

As human beings, we simply haven't remembered yet that we can trust in miracles.

ço·ço·ço·ço

## Mid-August, 2005

It was about a month before my 50th birthday. I like to think that I was only mildly ambivalent about it, but the truth is, those inevitable lines around my eyes were willing to reveal more than I was. Yet, I recognized 50 as an important milestone. How to celebrate my half-century on this planet was something I'd been kicking around for a couple of months when an employee finishing up her last day with us, appeared in my doorway.

"Rebecca," she said, "I have a parting gift for you."

Over the years I've learned to be cautious about gifts from departing employees. This particular employee was talented, bright, highly educated, yet eternally malcontent in her role with us. It simply wasn't a good fit. I was happy to see her make the decision to free herself, and find a new direction.

She went on to say, "You and I are about the same age—" at which point I briefly stopped listening. I had zealously guarded my age. How could she know that I was approaching 50?

"—and several years ago I had my horoscope done."

I almost snorted. It was all I could do to hold back the words *horoscope? Really!*

"I know, I know," she said, waving her hand, "it sounds silly. But, I tell you, it changed my life. And now that I'm about to turn 50, I'm going to have it done, again. I think you should too. Here's the name of my astrologer," she said, thrusting a carefully printed piece of paper into my hand. "*Do it, Rebecca,*" she urged. "I promise it will change your life."

She gave me a hug, and although I had never felt close to this woman, I honestly loved her in that moment. I loved her for caring; loved her for knowing that approaching 50 was a big deal.

Over the next several days my (now) former employee's words kept returning to me, and each time I played back the scene, it became more and more incongruent. She was a pragmatic, concrete woman. Yet, she had earnestly recommended something as 'new age' as meeting with an astrologer. Horoscopes for me were something we used to scan avidly in the daily newspaper back in the seventies, and then use as one-liners at clubs.

Yet, the idea was certainly different from any I'd had.

While I didn't know it, the time had come. My spiritual guides were doing everything possible to get my attention. That they used a sober-minded, in-the-box Catholic to deliver their message is wonderfully ironic, and just one example of their keenly divine sense of humor, as well as their earnest commitment to my welfare. It was so remotely unlikely to me that a horoscope reading would in any way 'change my life'.

Still, I was intrigued enough to make the call. After exchanging several voice mail messages it became clear that our schedules simply would not link up. It was with a real sense of disappointment that I dropped the idea of a reading. The very next day my friend Joyce heard a well-known psychic and spiritual healer on talk radio. Before I knew it, Joyce had arranged appointments for us with a highly recommended 'intuitive astrologer'.

**September 29, 2005 — My 50th Birthday**
Filled with a mixture of skepticism, curiosity, and sense of adventure, Joyce and I waited in the lobby of a popular health club for our appointment with Nancy, the 'intuitive astrologer'. We had no idea what to expect and were even a bit unclear as to how she would know us. Or we, her. Or even what all a 'reading' would involve.
When Nancy came through the doors of the crowded lobby, she walked directly over to us without hesitation. Impressive, I thought. Yet, I reserved the right to remain skeptical. We found a comfortable place to sit and talk, and I wondered how the session would begin. Nancy pulled out our charts, smoothed them both against the flat of the table, then turned to me and said, "Rebecca, you've been depressed lately about your mother's passing."

It was a statement, not a question. My mother had passed in 1981 and while some years had been better than others, I'd nursed that loss for a quarter of a century. Nancy went on to explain that my mother was present with us, and wanted me to know how much she loved me.

"Your mother," Nancy continued, "will sometimes visit you in the form of a scent, like perfume—oh, no, she's correcting me. It's the scent of a flower, or sometimes she will come to you as a bird—so, be watching for this. She wants you to know she is close."

I was enthralled. Nancy went back and forth between Joyce and me, sharing planetary insights, touching on memories to establish credibility, and interpreting messages from my mother, the angels, and other spiritual beings.

As the year following that first reading progressed I began to open up to the idea that the universe, or natural order of things was far different than I had believed it to be. Emotional health, spiritual wealth and physical well-being became more important to me once I realized that God is as much in us as external to us.

The light of remembering had begun.

**April, 2006**
I was sofa-napping on a rainy Saturday in April about six months after my session with Nancy. Spring was late that year. The rain was turning to snow. I was the only one in the house. All the windows and doors were closed. I hadn't fully dropped into sleep when I caught a whiff of something sweet. My heart grew soft with nostalgia. Lilac perhaps? Lilly of the valley? I couldn't tell. Where could such a scent come from?

My cat, Tasha who had been sleeping at my feet suddenly raised her head and sniffed. Then she rotated her head slowly as if she were watching something I could not see. The smell grew stronger. My fingers and toes tingled, and the hair on my arms stood stiff as I realized this was a visitation from my mother. After a moment, the smell began to fade, and the hair on my arms relaxed as if it were being stroked back into place.

It was so completely surreal, I was barely able to whisper, "is it you?" And then it was over.

**September 29, 2006**
A year later on my 51st birthday, Joyce and I met with Nancy again. One of the first things Nancy remarked about was how much more vibrant we were. Our auras were glowing, our vibrations were significantly higher, and there was an openness about us. I can't say that I actually understood what all that meant, but I knew it was a positive thing.

Toward the end of this session, Nancy told me that I needed to open up to a significant change with my work. My instinct told me she was right. At that time I was the manager of doctoral advising for a well-known university. I had been growing increasingly bored in my professional role but didn't know how to solve it. I had a good job. I did it well. By any definition, I was a professional success. Yet, I felt guilty about the boredom; about wanting more. I didn't know how to change the situation or even whether I had the right to try to change it. Privately, and primarily on a subconscious level, I believed that I had reached my professional peak.

In the late sixties, singer Peggy Lee released a song written by Stoller & Leiber entitled, *Is That All There Is*. The song derives from the story *Disillusionment* written by Thomas Mann, who experiences a series of tragedies throughout his life, and each time is left effete and incomplete, feeling that nothing will ever really impact him in either a positive or negative way. This is how I felt about my job, and at times, my life. Psychologists might describe this feeling as the general state of someone who is diagnosed with dysthymic disorder, a low-to-moderate level of depression that is persistent for more than two years, resistant to treatment, and can lead to major depression.
So, it's not surprising that I didn't want to talk about a possible job change. I kept trying to reroute the conversation.

But Nancy wouldn't be rerouted. "Rebecca, you've done so much healing in the area of your Mom," she said, "and your workplace for you represents your family. With all your healing, I hate to say it, but you're kind of done. So, if you stay there, you either have to find something new to be passionate about—find a way to rekindle your interest—or you have to leave. Because the way things are now, you're already done there."

"But I'm not *ready* to leave," I protested.

Nancy dipped her head and studied my chart before she continued. "Your work situation really underscores for you a feeling of not knowing who or where you are. It holds that vibration for you," she said. "So your challenge is to invite in clarity there. Have you thought about what else you can do?"

I shook my head.

"You're a good manager," she continued, "but I think you're tired of it. It would be nice if you could step back into a non-management role."

"I do have some desire to be an independent contributor," I admitted.

After more discussion she said, "next year will bring some opportunity for you to discover more about what's next for you. Keep in mind that your PhD isn't the only thing you've got going for you." She stopped to frown at my chart making little marks and diagrams I didn't understand. "The door is open for a lot of possibilities here," she added, nodding her head.

Then she looked directly at me. "But Rebecca, you *are* going to come into some kind of transition. There's something here in the creative part that I don't quite understand, and I really feel like you need to do something that allows you to retreat or hide for a year or so—"

This sounded so appealing to me, I agreed with her wholeheartedly.
"I mean there's *something*—" she hesitated, then continued, "but I just feel like if you start to let God know that you're available, it will come to you. And, I encourage you to start writing."

"I haven't written in years," I said.

"I know, and this is where you've placed your karma so it takes effort. You take the path of least resistance right now, so to write would take a lot of focus."

"But I think you're telling me to get going with that."

"Exactly!" she agreed. "And, the things you think you're going to write about," she paused to smile, "well, that's not what you're going to write about at all."

"You know," I told her, "I've even created a writing space for myself up in my loft in the hope that one day I will write again. I've never used it, but my cats go there and wait for me."

"Really, they know! Oh, how interesting! Yes," she nodded looking at my chart, "you're going to end up doing something really different. Just very different. But you're not ready for it, so it doesn't pay to talk about it, yet."

I knew she was right that something needed to change. Yet it terrified me. To hear her talk about a different kind of future was far more frightening to me than exciting. I was terribly, terribly stuck.

It was some of the worst kind of stuck. I loved my organization; I loved what we stood for and the fact that we were pioneers on the cutting edge of our industry. But my job was vastly unfulfilling.

It tore at me.

*"...change is the constant, the signal for rebirth, the egg of the Phoenix."*
— Christina Baldwin

# *Changes*

**November, 2006**

A month and a half later, Linda, my vice president suggested lunch. We walked across the street to a nearby restaurant. It was crowded, noisy and unappealing. I watched Linda take in the total lack of privacy, the noise level, the limited space, and noted the way her face flickered. *Uh-oh*, I thought. This meant we had something serious to talk about. We briefly considered walking to another restaurant when Linda spied a corner space at the bar on the far side of the restaurant that would provide a reasonable amount of privacy.

About mid-way through lunch Linda explained in a respectful and transparent manner that my position would be changing to a sales manager role. This meant that my expertise in doctoral education would no longer be essential.

"So, we need to talk about your options, here," she said. "First, of course is the option of you going into this changed role. Is this something you want to do?"

Without thinking I heard myself exclaim, *"No!"*

It was professional suicide. Yet, frankly, I felt I owed her the truth. But my conviction was not without fear. When I realized I had just told my manager I didn't want my job, I felt as if I might literally fall off the bar stool.

At the time of this meeting, Linda and I genuinely liked each other, held mutual respect for each other—even admiration, but often saw different sides of the elephant. She was my manager, and a vice president, so you get the idea which way things usually went. I had already done a sales stint with my organization. I had no interest in going backward.

Linda leaned forward and said, "Well, thanks for being honest with me, Rebecca, and this is what I really get excited about because now we have the opportunity to create a new role for you in the organization."

I sat back and allowed the full impact of her words to settle around me. My organization was going to let me design a new, custom-made position! As I listened to her, it became apparent that in order to do this, I would need to discover an unmet need, explain why it was important, and demonstrate how I could help our organization meet it. It was a true opportunity for innovation. It was also a testament to who we are as an organization, as well as to Linda and her integrity as an executive, leader, and human being.

Emily Dickinson wrote a poem that begins, "I dwell in possibility." I've used that opening line in presentations very effectively. I've used it to inspire teams. I even used it in my dissertation. When I'm at the top of my game, the idea of having many possibilities is romantic, exciting and intellectually stimulating. But, in recent weeks I had felt myself slipping back into the ter-rifying grip of depression.

Depression is something I've struggled with all of my adult life. With depression comes an inability to care, to corral any drive and move something new forward. New things require creativity. I knew the appropriate reaction to this opportunity was to feel excitement about the infinite possibilities. Yet it translated as some of the worst kind of pressure.

How was I ever going to develop something new? I was burned out. Crisped. Ash.

# Bloodroot

Brittle world
like standing a puzzle on end
to watch the white-on-white
pieces fall, clueless

Cue-less as the bloodroot
whose white petals
hide treacherous roots
that bleed beneath the surface
Blunt aspiration

Depression arrived like an unexpected guest when I was in my mid-thirties. Guests can be a wonderful experience, yet no matter how well-behaved the guest, or how excited we are to have guests, it takes effort. We almost always end up changing or in some way adjusting our routines to accommodate our guests.

It was 1987. In those days, no one talked openly about depression. Over time I learned that I was a high-functioning depressive. For the most part it did not interfere with work. Yet it crept around like a glacier crowding out a little more of my social life each day. I would make excuses to get out of dinner, or a Saturday morning brunch, or dates with interesting (and sometimes not-so-interesting) men without realizing it was becoming a pattern.

After awhile it was not satisfied with just curbing my social life. Depression was like a grape juice stain on satin; it just kept spreading and spreading until no color, no soft curves, no grassy knolls remained. The air was always thin and my breathing became permanently shallow. The worst was the inability to feel passionate about much of anything. On occasion the seemingly immutable despondency which left me numb would lift, only to be replaced by such a deep sadness, that I would weep ceaselessly. It felt as though I was crying for a thousand lifetimes.

It came and went like this over a period of twenty years. Each major tussle with depression was followed by a persistent low-to-moderate depression that allowed me to function at a reasonable, and even high level, but my ability to experience joy was significantly compromised.

One winter day in 2002, the inevitable happened. The "Big D" as I called it in my stronger moments, crossed over the line—broke all our tacit agreements and crawled into my workplace. It began with wet eyes. I kept dabbing them but they were like two pools fueled by natural springs. When the dabbing couldn't dam the overflow, I was both concerned and embarrassed. My desk was located in a public place so I fled to the sanctuary of the wellness room where I lay back in the recliner and cried.

Well, wailed, actually. What had begun as a silent leaking magnified as the moments passed. The front of my shirt was wet from tears, and my heart ached so hard I thought it would just turn over and give up. My head raged with splintering pain and worst of all, my throat burned from trying to keep my *panicked-animals-running-from-a-forest-fire* honking sounds from being heard.

This went on for over an hour. I could hear people walk up to the door, and then hesitate. I would stuff my hand into my mouth to try to quiet the sounds. If discovered, I thought I would die of embarrassment. Yet, each time I heard the soft shuffling of receding footfalls, it reinforced my feeling of isolation, of there being absolutely no help for this, and the honking tears would return with a vengeance.

When I thought I could finally speak, I flipped open my cell phone and called Ilene, a work colleague who was also a friend. But when she answered, all I could do was cry into the phone and whisper "wellness room."

Ilene is a shockingly verbal, warm-hearted friend who can be wonderfully wise at just the right moment. She is entirely forthright, and will give you the shirt off her back if you need it. She knew I was having some issues with depression, and this made it safe to call her. Ilene arrived at the wellness room with all the fierceness of a warrior ready to do battle or say grace.

She took one look at me and commanded, "Give me your hand."

I drove to my doctor's office only to find that my doctor was on vacation. No one knew what to do with me. Their faces said, *oh my gosh, there's a woman standing in the lobby crying and making animal sounds* (yes, sadly, the animal sounds had returned). It was late in the day. Almost everyone had gone home. They were able to dig up an internist who was well-intentioned but she had no clue what to do for me, so she connected me to the 800-help line associated with my medical insurance, where I was promptly put on hold.

Three years later in late December 2005, about two months after my first horoscope reading, my friend Joyce dropped by and found me so thoroughly depressed, I could barely respond to her. I had tried everything. Nothing would release me from the icy grip. Desperate to help me, she suggested we send an email to the Healing Pen Pal Program, a group of advanced healing students working with well-known psychic Echo Bodine. The healing pen pal network sends absentee healing to those who request it, for 15 days at a time. I had no faith that anything like this could make a difference. But I had nothing (and everything!) to lose.

There is no way to explain this scientifically. I can only say that less than twenty-four hours after sending an email request for help, I began to feel a shift. Within the month, I was able to introduce new routines into my life which focused on physical health and spiritual and emotional wellness.

If I were to sum up what I've written thus far in one sentence, I would say that I could not find my voice; that is, I hadn't remembered who I was, or why I chose to come into this lifetime, and this caused me to feel so separate from myself that I experienced erratic, reoccurring bouts of depression.

But they tell me that it's time now to get to the story of transformation!

### Trish — March, 2006

During lunch one day I found myself sharing the story of my two readings with Trish, a colleague with whom I had been working for about a year. The moment Trish and I met, we both experienced a strong sense of déjà vu—as if we had met before. She had a fresh naturalness that drew me in. It was no surprise that we hired her. I found her easy to trust and uplifting to be around.

As I began to tell her about my two readings with Nancy, it was as if some kind of flush mechanism was activated. My throat became a vortex of run-on sentences, and although I trusted her, the entire time I was talking my brain flashed this neon sign that screamed, *what will she think of you??*

When it was over, Trish smiled a bit thoughtfully and commented that she had spiritual abilities, too and could feel my mother's presence with us. "Your Mother is nodding her head and wants you to know she agrees with all that Nancy told you," she said. During dessert Trish talked briefly about her own ability to communicate with 'the other side'. She was entirely credible.

Several weeks later Trish announced she was leaving to start her own business as a life coach. Although we hadn't worked nearly as closely together as I would have liked, an unusual feeling of separation settled over me—a definite sense of loss. She said something about becoming a *certified energetic practitioner*; words which had no meaning to me, but it didn't matter. I was certain she would be successful.

Trish had found her light.

*"...we spend far too much time and energy contemplating our inadequacies. We forget that we are all perfect in our imperfection."*

— Kate Dillon

# *Awakening*

**November 6, 2006**

Given my current state, how was I ever going to discover an unmet need within my organization and develop something new?

In some ways, this moment in time represents every woman's greatest fears. I was alone, solely dependent on myself. I was compensated at a generous level that would take time, patience and clarity to match if I were to leave my current place of employment. I was over 50; clearly a stereotype I was having some difficulty with. I was childless by choice, my social network was very small, and the creeping glacier of depression had an unremitting hold on me—for how long this time? This is what I saw when I took inventory of my life.

My family doctor would say from time to time, "Rebecca, stoic is stupid. People die of stoicism because they think it's wrong to ask for help."

So, after a weekend of agonizing about my unknown future (as if there are ever any guarantees!) and my questionable ability to focus through the glacier of depression, I realized it was time to 'call in the troops'—a phrase that kept coming to me, over and over. I didn't know for certain what it meant. It was simply a feeling I had—a kind of knowing that it was time to stop being a solitary soldier, and invite help. When Monday morning came, I awoke with a new thought. I would ask Linda to approve funding for coaching sessions with Trish!

To my great relief, when I broached the subject, Linda smiled broadly and immediately agreed. "I've used her myself," she said. "This will be a great experience—I'm excited for you!"

**Session One out of Six — November 14, 2006**
When I showed up at Trish's doorstep, I was a wreck; wild-eyed about every ticking moment which drew me further away from the safety of steady employment. I did not yet know that my subconscious fear of having reached my professional peak had effectively blinded me to all the possibilities that lay before me. Fear was a relentless overseer.

"What's *wrong* with me?" I cried.

"You're grieving," she answered, her face as solemn as her voice. "It's as if you're mourning the loss of children. Let's look at why it feels that way," she suggested.

So true. In the eleven years I'd been with my organization, we grew from fledgling inexperience to considerable success. Although I had no passion remaining for my current job, I was passionate and proud about the growth of my organization, and what we stood for. I didn't trust that I could go somewhere else and be successful because I was unclear about myself, both privately and professionally.

*Wow, is she ever good!* I thought. *I've been inside her house for less than five minutes and already I have clarity.* Clarity about the past, perhaps, but not a clue what to do, next.

"Have you ever had a session like this?" Trish asked.

I wasn't sure what she meant, so I said, "I don't know what we're going to do."

"We're going to listen to your spiritual guides," she told me.

*Spiritual guides?* It sounded like Native American folklore to me.

Then she asked, "Did your mother like purple irises?" I nodded. Indeed, irises had been among her favorite flowers. "Well, the room is filled with purple irises, and this is her way of letting you know she is here."

In that moment I knew I had arrived at a new truth, and that what I would learn through my work with Trish would take me out of my darkness. As I opened to this new experience, the room grew bright with a light I could not see.

# Awakening

When the blind see
and the deaf hear
Heaven has opened her doors.

"And, now," Trish said, "they're telling me it's time to get practical. They're showing me that you're blocked. You are judging yourself harshly for being unable to see your next professional move. They want us to begin our work together by introducing you to an important truth which is that the universe is a loving place where there is no judgment; only opportunities and love."

"You are being harder on yourself than you would ever be on others," she continued. "They want to help you learn to love yourself by imagining a world in which love flows from one ending to the next beginning."

*"...one doesn't discover new lands without consenting to lose sight of the shore for a very long time."*

— Andre Gide (1869-1951)

# *Discovery*

What remains is to tell you what I learned, and how I learned it, over the year that followed.

Most importantly, I learned that we are created in love, to love and be loved. Every one of us has a 'network' of angels, spiritual guides and other spiritual beings who are with us, allegiant and wise. They watch over us, guide us, and protect us. We are all born into this world with natural gifts and talents, some of which we can turn into skills, and all of which we can use, if we choose, to fulfill our life's purpose—the purpose we agreed to, prior to coming into this world.

By 'life's purpose', I don't mean to imply that we sign up for only one purpose in life. Before coming into this world we sign up for a range of things, typically because our abilities, gifts, and cumulative learning facilitates a great deal of choice in terms of purpose. So, I might be a healer, a writer, a teacher, a leader, a philosopher all of which I can use to fulfill my life's purpose.

Our spiritual guides can help us with all the mysteries of life, from how to change the electrical wiring in the kitchen, to finding a post office in a strange neighborhood, to advising us about what we might charge for consulting fees. And, I've called on them for all of these things.

But most importantly, they helped me unwind myself until I could love again.

By the end of my first session with Trish I understood that I was operating from a place of great, but superficial fear. This fear caused me to believe intellectually that I wanted things to remain the same. But my heart, which always desires to do meaningful work, longed for change. It was a troubling dichotomy.

My guides taught me that the heart is mightier than the head. My heart's desire for more meaningful work was already causing things to change. I was still stuck, to be sure. But I could feel the magnitude—the grand design of how the universe responds to what we really want. And, what we really want is to be involved in 'work' that allows us to fulfill the life purpose we agreed to, prior to coming into the world.

As much as this may seemingly not be consonant with the Christian teachings that have always guided my belief system, it seems undeniable that we live many lifetimes. We do this to learn lessons. As we learn lessons, our soul (or higher consciousness) gains wisdom, and we move deeper into what I call the Light, which is the love that streams unceasingly from God. We become lighter and brighter as we learn the lessons we are intended to learn; all of which are lessons of love.

I have been using the term 'God' and will continue to use it because it is the term I am most comfortable with. But I believe it does not matter what term we use; God, Source, Allah, Consciousness, the Universe, you choose. For me, embracing these spiritual truths has deepened my faith in God.

Pain, fear, and all other negative experiences result from conflict between our human spirituality and our ego. Pierre Teilhard de Chardin (1881-1955) was a visionary French Jesuit, paleontologist, biologist, and philosopher, who spent the bulk of his life trying to integrate religious experience with natural science. He is credited with having said, "I am a spiritual being who is currently engaged in a human experience." (Wall translation, 1975).

The truth is, we are *all* spiritual beings engaged in a human experience. Upon being born, our humanness required that we learn the ways of being human, including adapting to the gift of a body that facilitates a pleasurable, tactual experience.
But, I'm getting ahead of myself.

As a part of our first session, Trish helped me discover that I needed to love myself more, let go of the impossibly high standards I'd set for myself, and free myself from the resulting harsh self-judgment when I couldn't meet those standards. She gave me homework that included interviewing people about my attributes.

"By attributes, I mean just the positive things," she clarified. "Then spend some quiet moments and think about whether you agree with them. Be prepared to defend any attribute you disagree with," she warned.

The idea made me squirm. Finally I said, "Trish, "you see me differently than others."

"Really?" This with a raised eyebrow. "I don't believe that's true, and this is your chance to find out."

Throughout our session Trish would assume different positions. Sometimes she moved around the room. Sometimes she squatted. Most often, she sat cross-legged on a floor pillow in front of me making movements with her hands that looked almost as if she were sewing invisible cloth. Sometimes it seemed as if the thread was very, very long and it would take an exaggerated movement to pull it all through. Other times, I noticed that the "thread" was very short. She explained that these movements were a sort of psychic surgery that would help to remove toxins from my body and help me heal.

"How much time do you have to create this new position?" Trish asked.

I shrugged. "We didn't define it, but you know Linda. She moves fast. My guess is that I have until about the end of the year. And even that will seem like an eternity given the fast pace of our work environment."

Trish nodded. "Yes, they're telling me your timeframe is about eight or nine weeks. One of the things that will help Linda feel assured that you're working on it is to give her regular updates. Communicate up."

I didn't say it out loud but this felt impossible. I couldn't imagine what I would tell Linda. Perhaps something like, "Linda, I'd just like to give you a quick update. My first session with Trish was wonderful. I cried the entire time, walked away from it exhausted, and have no idea what to do next with my career. But oh, by-the-way, my dead mother says hello..." Something like that, perhaps?

"Just tell her how much you appreciate her support and that you're making good progress," Trish counseled, and I wondered if she could read my mind, or just how much of my thoughts the guides actually share with her.

At this point in our session, Trish asked if I had any questions, and I burst out laughing. *Did I have any questions?!*

She giggled with me and said, "Let's deal with a couple of those questions now."

Who are my guides, I wanted to know.

Is there anyone else, I wondered.

How did my mother fit into all of this?

"They tell me you're an old soul," Trish said. "You've had many, many lives dating back to the Stone Age."

This was strangely comforting, and yet not at all. To be in crisis the way I was, and then find out I'm an old soul made me wonder what I'd been learning over the centuries—or more to the point, what I hadn't been learning!

"You have an abundance of support," Trish continued. "For example, you have several ascended masters working with you."

*Ascended masters?* As with spiritual guides, this was another concept with terminology I did not understand.

"Yes. Ascended masters are those who were once human, are now ascended, and who are known as saints as a result of their earthly lives. They are geared toward action, missions, or the implementation of something."

The two ascended masters who chose to reveal themselves to me that day were St. Bernard, and Mother Teresa. Both were specifically focused on working with me in my current state of crisis.

"The healing for you," Trish said, "is to find the connecting thread; what do you have in common with Mother Teresa and St. Bernard?"

Through my research I learned that St. Bernard was a French Abbot in the twelfth century. He has been described as noble of nature, tender in his dealings with others, and possessing a genuine humility. An eloquent preacher, he was known for his mellifluous voice and manner that spoke to the hearts rather than the heads of humanity. He was both poet and scholar.

Mother Teresa is well-known today as one of recent history's most consummate conflict managers. She was superb in the practice of manifestation and managed to repeatedly accomplish the impossible.

What did I have in common with these two? I couldn't begin to guess.

"And now," Trish said, "because you are ready, and because she is an integral part of your support system, they want to help you understand your deep attachment to your mother."

The year was 1659. I was twelve and recently orphaned. With no known relatives, I was given to a family who had no children. But they were cold. So cold that I chose to run away, even though I knew I would likely not survive long out in the world on my own. Within a week's time, my hair turned white. My mother found me starving, filthy, and wraithlike, stealing garbage from the back of the bakery next to the textile shop she owned with her mother.

She took me in, taught me to sew, and brought me into the family business which was to fashion intricate sails for many of the ships that sailed in and out of port. My mother never married in that lifetime, and instead devoted herself to me. That bond was so strong we agreed to never be separated again.

"When you made the decision to come into this life," Trish continued, "you asked your mother to do this life with you. She declined saying she was done with her earthly lives. But you persisted, clear that you needed her in order to complete your purpose for this lifetime. Although she did not want to do another earthly life, she eventually agreed to be your mother. As a result, she 'holds the container of your life'."

This phrase meant nothing to me, so I asked for clarification. But Trish and my guides were clear that this was a phrase I would have to learn to understand on my own.

"Oh, this is interesting," she continued. "Every night while you're in dream state, you leave your body to join your mother. This is not unusual. Many people leave their body in dream state. Your struggle is that you hate to return to your body—"

"You're so fortunate, Rebecca," Trish told me, breaking from the story. "Your mother is a very together soul. Just because someone has passed doesn't necessarily make them 'clear'. I've seen a lot of 'unclear' parents who have passed and are trying to help their children. Oh!—" she broke off in surprise. "She tells me she is a spiritual guide for women in prison. She wants to make it clear that she is not *your* spiritual guide. But she is with you in love, always. In fact, sometimes she comes to you as a bird."

*"... The most beautiful experience we can have is the mysterious —*
*the fundamental emotion which stands at the cradle of true art and*
*true science."*
— Albert Einstein from *Living Philosophies,* 1931

# *Spiritual Guides*

Over the next hour I learned that Thomas is my 'lead' spiritual guide. Trish described him as lighthearted, an easy sense of humor, gravely deep, with amazing red hair. He has been with me throughout all of my lifetimes, and will always be with me. He was assigned to me when I was a new soul for many reasons that I don't understand, but one of them is because I was born with the soul of a poet.

Thomas is a scholar, a teacher and guides a great deal of my poetry. There were two others who came forward; Stephen and Violet. In time, additional guides would come forward, as I passed through a number of evolutionary stages; each one a sort of transformation.

"They are applauding you," Trish sighed, clapping her hand over her heart. "They celebrate the life you've lived, and it's important for you to know this. Part of your unrest is because it's time to make a change. Before you came into this world, you knew you were going to need a little extra 'push' to take the next step. So, you made an agreement with your guides that if you hadn't begun this next phase by now, they were to become more obvious—start pushing your buttons, so to speak, to wake you up spiritually and help you move forward."

"You see, Rebecca," she continued, "we all have free will. So, our guides can only counsel us. We can always choose not to keep our agreements."

# Spirit Guide

He waits
among purple iris
and white gardenias
Jesus-like with his
sandaled feet
and red beard

That's how I imagine him
dark nights
when coruscating light
toys with tired eyes
a sense so faithless,
I wonder
about truth

So what do I trust,
My eyes?
Or the knowing in my heart
that Thomas comes to me,
walking through the purple iris
and white gardenias
talking in a language
calibrated just for us

Soon after this session I realized that my guides had indeed been coming forward in ways that I had noticed, yet not noticed. For example, each night as I fell asleep soon after I moved into my townhome in 2004, the sound of soft murmuring brushed up against me, barely noticeable. I could never discover where it was coming from, and after several months, the murmurings went away.

Every soul has a unique personality; a fusion of attributes. Trish asked my guides if I could be introduced to my soul's personality so that I would better understand my true self. "It might begin to ease your harsh self-judgment," she explained to me. My guides agreed.

"You are a warrior," Trish began, her head tipped slightly to the right as she listened intently to my guides. "Tenacious and brave." She raised a closed fist and gently tapped it against her heart. "They're showing me this movement," she explained. "A warrior in touch with your heart."

I didn't understand the message, and didn't much like hearing that I was a warrior. Where was the gentleness? Where was the tenderness and peace I so desperately craved? "Isn't there anything positive?" I whimpered tearfully.

Trish looked surprised, "Positive? You don't think of this as positive?" She broke off to listen, and then continued. "You are a warrior for peace. Kind, gentle, funny and mysterious. And when you are balanced, you have the ability to inspire people to new levels of insight."

This was starting to sound better.

"You are also an empath. That's what they mean by *in touch with your heart.* Your empath is stronger than your warrior but you don't feel her because she's an empath, and therefore does not have her own strong personality. Your empath works with your warrior to help you use courage and bravery for peace and change. Your challenge is to keep your warrior and your empath balanced. Too much warrior and you have no peace. Too much empath and you simply entrain to everyone else, and cannot make yourself heard or implement change."

Trish gave in to a deep-throated chuckle. "Rebecca, they're showing me building blocks; you know, plastic building blocks for children, and they're playing with them, making formations that are smooth, ordered and without chaos. But there's something different. Instead of primary colors, these building blocks are lovely pastel shades. Let me ask about the significance of this image."

Oh, how I wished I could see what Trish saw!

"They told me that, just as building blocks have a specific pattern or place in order to build something, they are playing with them to assure us both that the pieces are falling into place for you. The pastel shades are a reflection of your true peaceful nature. Right now, your guides are gleefully building objects with the pastel-colored blocks, laughing and clasping their hands together in short bursts of applause because you have made such a strong connection with them today."

My own joy began to gurgle up when I heard this. From that day to this, when I think of my guides, the first impression I receive is three roly-poly beings in long robes tumbling over each other; gleefully carefree. It's their personalized message to me to find joy. To look for, and honor the lighter moments of life.

"And now," Trish said, drawing our first session to a close with words I would hear often over the next twelve months, "we are complete."

A good thing, too! I'd slogged through all the Kleenex, and still my cheeks were wet. My energy level had dropped to below exhausted. Trish counseled me to drink a lot of water throughout the remainder of the day.

"They want you to know that you've done a tremendous amount of healing over the last two hours."

How strange, I remember thinking. How strange to think of the last two hours as healing. Which gives you an idea of just how disconnected I had been from my own need and desire to heal and be whole.

*"...I am the miracle."*
— Buddha

# *Unfolding*

In the week that followed, I asked three people to give me feedback about my attributes. I found it difficult to ask and had to swallow hard, each time I did it. I wasn't afraid of what I would hear. No matter how much my employees might have wanted me to be different, I knew they believed I cared about them. So, I didn't think I would hear bad things, or that they would struggle to find good things to say. What was so difficult about this assignment was 1) to *ask* them to share with me, 2) and then to believe them. Believing them was the hardest. I could believe they *meant* what they said. What I had trouble believing was that they were *right*.

Their feedback was supportive, appreciative, and in some cases, even flattering. I liked hearing how they described me. What I was most surprised about was how much they appeared to want to tell me good things about myself. I *wanted* to believe them yet had trouble doing so. To be clear, it wasn't that I thought they were lying. My self-esteem was at an all-time low, and I simply thought they were seeing good things in me that in fact weren't really there.

Late in the week I was wrapping up a meeting with a young woman who in my opinion had a tremendous amount of potential, yet often displayed an unintentionally brusque manner. I had been so impressed with her during her interview that I had actually bumped another candidate in order to hire her. But a few weeks after she started, I wondered if I had made a mistake. This new employee just made the work disappear. Everything she touched took only moments to complete. What is the problem, you ask? Well, the problem was that her communication style was just as quantum.

One day she said to me, "Rebecca, I'm going out of my mind. I've just got to have more to do." Soon after that, I was able to offer a handful of people the opportunity to give seminar presentations on a regular basis. It meant they had to be willing to train, practice and sharpen their presentation skills, and meet certain protocols. When my 'quantum' employee asked to be a part of the presentation team, my heart sank. Her abbreviated communication style was at such odds with the skills and qualities required of a good presenter, I just couldn't see how it would ever work.

I was about to decline when it felt as if someone was lifting my chin, forcing me to look directly into this employee's eyes. There, I saw true openness. She was making herself vulnerable to me; something that was clearly not easy for her to do. The moment seemed endless while I wondered what to say or do, when she spoke first. "Rebecca," she said solemnly, "I promise I will knock your socks off."

And she did. She worked harder than anyone I've ever seen. When we began working together on the project, she lacked confidence, she had poor eye contact, her voice was sometimes difficult to listen to, her posture was hunched, and she second-guessed everything she said and did. She was trying to please me. We are never going to get there this way, I thought.

I sat down with her and talked about the difference between trying to please me, and simply pleasing herself. I knew her standards were at least as high as mine, so if she just tried to please herself instead guessing about what would please me, I believed she would be successful. I watched this woman park her ego, put away her pride and listen to every suggestion I gave her. What I enjoyed most about watching this transformation was how proud she was of herself; genuinely pleased with what she had accomplished. And she had a right to be!

Now, it was my turn to be vulnerable with her. "I wonder," I began, "if you would be willing to give me some feedback."

Her eyes filled with tears, and she said quietly, "You're the only one who's ever been willing to mentor me, and the most important thing you have taught me is that sometimes it's important to let someone else win."

The empath in me flipped a series of somersaults and floated lightly to the ground like a ballerina. There was some gentleness in me, after all!

༜༜༜༜

Between sessions there were two things that demanded most of my time. The first was curling up in a ball as tight as possible while I wept. Was I trying to make myself invisible? Was I protecting my core? Was this a new Yoga technique and I just didn't know it?

The second was walking. Not far from my home is an enchanting walking path that winds for two-and-a-half miles around a lovely lake, through woods, and over creeks. At times the woods are so thick you can't see the lake at all. Two-and-a-half miles proved not quite long enough to loosen the grip of depression, and just long enough to suffer the bitter kiss of an unforgiving November wind.

Each time I walked that path, my companion for the first mile was the grating, repetitious, chilling thought, I don't know *what* to do, I don't *know* what to do, I don't know what to *do*. I've only got nine weeks, [then] eight weeks, [then] seven weeks, [then] six weeks… who can change their entire career in just five weeks… *I don't know what to do'.*

The second mile was all about, 'tell me what to *do*, just tell me what to do, *damn-it*, just *tell* me what to do'. And finally, the last half mile was their turn. They would place a sort of 'knowing' in my heart. The 'knowing' was always the same. 'Tell us what you *want*, Rebecca'.

The day came when I realized I was not alone walking the path around the lake. I had the impression that someone or something was keeping me company. I wondered if I should be afraid. Whole sections of the path were entirely secluded. Was I in danger walking this path in broad daylight? Yet, it didn't feel like danger so much as it felt like I simply was not alone.

Making choices is difficult when you're depressed. It's much easier to simply let fear be in control. This is what Nancy meant when she said 'you take the path of least resistance right now'. But that day, I made an important choice to continue walking the lake; to trust that I was not in danger.

The heaviness lifted from my chest and I remember looking up to see a woodpecker in the tree above. It pecked and chattered, and then seemed to follow me around most of the lake. In fact, it seemed like a lot of birds, mostly woodpeckers, were hopping from tree-top to tree-top, keeping me company as I tread the path. I loved the physical reminder that I wasn't alone.

*"...the goal of spiritual practice is full recovery; and the only thing you need to recover from is a fractured sense of self.*
— Marianne Williamson

# *Letting Go*

### Session Two of Six — November 22, 2006

"The truth is—" that's as far as I got before I started to weep. "The truth is," I tried again, "I've spent two days curled up tight like a ball rocking and mewling like some kind of stray."

"But you've also been walking," Trish said looking off to the right as she does when 'they' are talking with her.

"Why can't I see this as the wonderful opportunity it is? Why can't I get excited about it? Instead, I just get scared," I was crying again. "I tried to give Linda an update but I couldn't even look her in the eyes. I'm so afraid she's going to catch on that I am immobilized by fear."

"Rebecca, did you ever watch the TV show, Wonder Woman?"

Laughter trickled up through my tears. It was such an unexpected change of subject. "Yes. I wanted to *be* her," I admitted.

"And do you remember her shield? She had a shield. It made a funny sound when she used it. The shield protected her from harm."

I nodded.

"Well every morning before you get out of bed, I want you to imagine that shield. You are going to shield yourself with wonder woman's shield, only find a way to make it your own. Most importantly, while this shield protects you from harm, it does not isolate you. When you imagine the shield coming over you, ask God to protect you so that you can do your highest and best in all things. By doing this, you will be able to stand in your own power. Shielding yourself creates the luxury of time and space to manage your thoughts and reactions. "

I loved it. I loved everything about it. More importantly, I believed it. This two-second effort has become a part of my daily routine, and it does wonders (pun intended)!

Over the course of the next hour my guides told me that I was caught up in believing something about myself that was no longer true, and it was keeping me from being able to see all the possibilities and opportunities that were present. They were referring to my imposter syndrome which feeds on self-doubt. To help me understand that I was not an imposter, they reminded me of specific occurrences in my life where I was (as they described via Trish) 'spectacularly successful'. Their message was 'you are authentic. You can trust yourself'.

They also pointed out how egotistical we often are as human beings. We equate a strong work ethic with setting the bar high and holding ourselves to higher expectations than we do others. It's the 'I'm the manager and that makes me responsible, so I have to do more, faster and better than everyone else'. Their message was that it is egotistical to expect more of ourselves than we do of others. It's fine to set the bar high. But we often don't realize that setting the bar higher for ourselves is one way of saying to the world, 'You will never be as good as me'.

I could feel myself open up to the idea of setting reasonable goals. Reasonable goals would help me feel more authentic, less out of my league, and reduce my harsh self-judgment. This was a lesson about emancipation. I thought of it as 'lightening up' and my breathing became easier.

"They're asking if you would like to have it removed," Trish told me.

"Have what removed?" I wasn't quite keeping up.

"The last vestiges of your imposter syndrome. If you think it serves some good, they'll leave it alone. Originally, your imposter syndrome helped you keep your ego in check. But you don't need that safety net anymore because your empath archetype has unfolded and is now partnering with your warrior archetype. So, if you want it gone, they're ready to clear you of it. It's time

43

for you to believe in your authentic self."

Incredulously I asked, "They can do that?"

Trish smiled. "They can do anything."

I felt instant and immeasurable relief as the self-doubt and feelings of inadequacy I had clung to for so long, dissolved.

*"...as soon as you trust yourself, you will know how to live."*
— Johann Wolfgang Goethe (1749-1832)

# *Trust*

**Session Three of Six — November 29**
Trish opened our third session with, "something has changed." Although I had been feeling stronger and more confident, this single statement detonated a legion of tears. With so many changes, I was, frankly, exhausted.

"Your guides have been working with you to help you unlearn certain things," she explained. "For example, one of the reasons you have such an emotional hold on your current job is because your family belief system taught that it's more important to have longevity at a job than to have longevity in a relationship."

Once she said it, I could see how true it was!

"So what has changed this week?" she prompted.

What had changed? I knew of three things. First, it had been profoundly rewarding to complete the last of my feedback assignment. Through it I found professional respect and even love. I learned that I have taught people to think more wisely, led people to be more courageous, and helped people heal. These truths, especially the last one, had a rebalancing effect on my self-esteem. I could trust myself to invest in people. I was a good manager after all!

Second, although I could have delayed it until my own transition was complete, I helped to facilitate the shift of half my direct reports to another manager. Several internal changes in our organizational structure suggested a change like this made good business sense. It was one step toward letting go of my current role, of forcing myself to move forward. Facilitating the implementation of a positive change reminded me how good it feels to build something. I could trust myself to put the good of the organization, and my direct reports, first.

The third change was that I had successfully employed some of the counsel provided by my guides about the art of entrainment. "When your empath is too strong," Trish warned, "she will cause you to entrain to others and be a pleaser. When she is balanced, you will know when you are to be the entrainer or entrainee. Much of your purpose right now is to entrain others to you."

During this session my guides became very specific. I was to start thinking of myself as 'Dr. Grant, the organizational development professional'. It was time for me to see myself in terms of my accomplishments so that I could believe in myself. With the imposter syndrome eradicated, this would be easier to do.

"They tell me you have a tendency to hold on to what you know, rather than to look for something new and challenging. This is partly because of your family teachings about job longevity. But, more importantly it is because persistence and fortitude are lessons you had to learn in this lifetime. You've had many lifetimes where you did not build up these skills. They want to assure you that you've successfully developed these skills very effectively. You've completed the assignment and learned the lessons of persistence and fortitude. You will always be able to trust yourself to stand your ground where appropriate. To 'go the distance'."

I could trust myself!

"Now, it's time to let in the light, feel the joy and move forward. You get to do something new, Rebecca! And, while you're doing that," she added, "it's time to pitch a job to Linda. You won't get it, but it's what they're calling 'divine practice'."

I started to quake.

*"...happiness is not a matter of intensity but of balance, order, rhythm and harmony."*

— Thomas Merton

# *Balance*

**Session four of six  — December 5, 2006**
"They're showing me that when you ran away at the age of twelve in 1659, you internalized it as failure. You knew it was a necessary choice, but defying the cultural norms was a 'bad thing'. Hiding, stealing food, sneaking around; all 'bad things'. In the end, anything short of standing your ground, regardless of the circumstances or consequences, feels like a failure to you. "

"So," she continued, "you find yourself *falling on your sword* a lot, so to speak, in order to stand your ground. In this lifetime, you've placed your integrity with standing your ground. But now that you've mastered the persistence challenge, they're suggesting you reframe it in this way—try thinking of it as 'running toward something' instead of 'running away'. That will help you recognize cues, nudges and opportunities more easily."

My body softened as everything cellular folded into alignment with her words. Between the subconscious belief that I was married to my job, and my need to stand my ground, I had backed myself into a corner that would not allow me to walk away from something, simply because I wanted to.

"There's more. They're going to really drive this home with you today, Rebecca. They want you to look at what actually happened, instead of seeing it through your filter. You've been thinking, 'I can't leave a perfectly good job'. To be accurate, you *can* leave a perfectly good job. And when you remove your filter of shame and failure, you can say to yourself, 'I work for a great organization, and give myself permission to continue moving forward on my professional journey'. Somehow you've internalized this opportunity as failure. Rebecca, there is no failure here." She was calm and low-throated as she spoke. Her eyes never wavered; ever focused on the space to the left of my head.

"Let's revisit the facts," she continued. "Linda said your job was being turned into a sales manager role. She asked you if you wanted to keep your job once it was recast. You were true to yourself and said 'no'. There is only courage in that action. And then what happened?  Did she thank you for your contribution and show you the door?  No!  She said, 'there's the drawing board. Go create something new'."

I knew Trish had stopped talking, but I was still back at *it's okay to want to leave my current job.*

Click. The idea was starting to take hold.

*It was okay to seek out challenge.*

Click.

*It was okay that Linda had recognized this before I did.*

Click.

*I was not the beneficiary of a hand-out. Linda was not giving me the opportunity to create a new role for myself because she felt sorry for me, or because I had failed. She was giving me this opportunity because I was a success. She and others trusted I would be creative and resourceful enough to identify an important, and as yet unmet need in the organization, and develop a plan.*

Click. Click. Click.

৯৯৯৯

"How did your pitch to Linda, go?" Trish asked, changing the subject abruptly, as often happens in our sessions.

I chuckled. "You won't believe this—or, maybe you already know?"

Trish shook her head to indicate she knew nothing.

"Well, I was getting ready to pitch her an idea when we ran into each other unexpectedly in the skyway. Before I could get a word out she told me she had a great idea for my new role."

"Did you like her idea?"

"Well, it scared me to death. I don't really think I'm qualified for it but I was so amazed that she saw me as someone who could do a job like that."

"So you opened up to it?"

"I don't think it will ever fly—" Trish started to raise an eyebrow but this time I was ready. "I'm pretty sure it isn't where the organization wants to place their attention right now, but we agreed to have lunch later this week and talk about it. In the meantime, I am to think about how she and I can pitch this position to others, since it's outside her decision-making area."

Trish jumped up and wrapped her arms around herself. "This is what they're showing me, Rebecca," she said. "They're hugging you, and the message is that because you opened up and were ready to pitch a position to her, you didn't have to. She felt your openness and that openness helped her to think creatively about a new role for you."

I loved the idea that by opening myself up, the biggest part of the challenge (pitching a job) just fell away. Opening up, or *unfolding* as Trish likes to call it, creates an entirely new energy and changes what will happen next.

I wanted to return to something Trish had talked about in one of our earlier sessions when she said that in my role as a peace person, I was a healer. What was that all about?
My guides suggested I think of myself as a bamboo bowl. They told me it might be helpful to go get a bamboo bowl, and that I could pick one up at Pier One or World Market (they are so handy!). The bamboo represents both flexibility and strength, analogous to the partnership between my empath and my warrior archetypes. The greatest strength is in my ability to be flexible, yet strong.

The bowl represents openness and possibility. Bowls have many uses. For example, they are utilitarian—they hold things. They are often used to mix ingredients to produce something different like salad, bread, cake. They can be used to serve divine purpose, such as a baptismal font, or a crock of essential oils.

When we become bowls, we let others 'toss things into our bowl'. Specifically, this might be the act of listening to someone. Phrased another way, this is a demonstration of empathy. Listening empathically is a form of validation. It allows others to be vulnerable with us. When we allow this, we help others recognize the ability to empower themselves, and their subconscious reaction is 'thank you for the gift of attention. I'm going to soar now'.

Ultimately, I've just described the phenomenon of emotional intelligence. The practice of emotional intelligence is to invest in others. And this is what my guides mean when they refer to me as a healer. As people heal, they make better decisions, guided by their heart as well as their intellect. In this way, we are all healers. Every human being has the ability to heal and be healed.

Bowls also metaphorically serve as sacred space in which new things are created. As people toss things into our bowl, those things mingle and re-emerge in the form of new ideas. This is the act of innovation that through co-creation produces new thoughts, ideas and solutions.

When we think of ourselves as a bowl, it is important to first shield ourselves and ask God to allow us to do our highest and best. In this way, if someone tosses something into your bowl that is not positive or helpful, it simply bounces back out. As I began to use this tool, it was helpful for me to visualize negativity as rocks. As 'rocks' were tossed into my bowl, I simply took a moment to visualize flipping my bowl over and dumping the rocks out. For every rock I dumped out, I replaced it with golden light.

# *Earthbound Spirits*

As was becoming our usual practice, Trish asked me if I had any questions. It occurred to me that I should ask about what was going on in my loft.

**Fall, 1981**
My townhome was built in 1981. The deed says 1982, but it's wrong. I know because in 1981 I was deeply in love with my soon-to-be husband. I was nearly 26. He was a tall, intellectual type with an attractive athletic build. He was mild-mannered, polite, had an amusing laugh that was slightly apologetic, and oh-so-distant. We could not have been more different. He was about eight years older than I, and was building a brilliant career. His parents were academicians. His world was one of accomplishment, learning, books, culture—he thought in terms of potential and possibilities. It was all new to me. I was in awe of the lifestyle as much as I was in love with the man.

In mid-September that year, my mother died of ovarian cancer. My mother and I made many mistakes in our 25 years together, as human beings will. Yet, I loved her more than I ever loved anyone. She was light to me and I often referred to her as my best friend. As a child, I would tan deeply and she would draw me into the sweetness of her arms, call me her little brown bear and tell me over and over that I had taught her to love.

When she died, I fell apart; sometimes in gargantuan chunks, and other times in little pieces so imperceptible, I didn't know they were slipping away. I threw myself into house hunting and getting married hoping to heal grief with excitement about the way my life was changing.

One day my fiancé and I ran across a sign in a lovely wooded area of the suburbs, followed by more signs. Eventually the signs led us to a row of townhouses in various stages of completion. The model home was nearly finished and open for viewing. We were both charmed. The flow was

wonderful; open yet warm. The back side of the house edged a wetlands sur-
rounded by tall oaks, a few ash, and thick underbrush that grew like sentinels
around a shallow pond. Beyond the pond we could see gently swaying
lengths of grass that bent in homage to the breeze. The blended sounds of
chickadees, gold finches, nuthatches, woodpeckers and red wing blackbirds
told us the wetlands were alive with wildlife. It was nothing short of sacred.

The townhome, as it turned out, was a bit too small for our plans and we
really preferred a single family home, so we walked away. Yet, it made a
lasting impression.

**1985**
Over the next couple of years I kept breaking until my husband couldn't take
it any longer. I came home one day and found a note on the bed. In it, he
tried to explain how much he needed peace. I couldn't understand what he
was saying. The concept of being peaceful was so remote, it presented no
value to me. All I knew was pain and anger. All I could remember or feel
was the opposite of peace. And worse, I had no desire for peace. It was that
meaningless to me.

A few months after he left, I began to write. There were voices in my head
and heart that would not be silenced. I didn't understand them, and the only
way to let them out was to write. I tried to write all the things I heard, but
they were elusive, even coy.

**July, 2004**
One morning in late July, 2004 I awoke with a new idea. I was going to buy
a home. I'd been renting apartments for twenty years with no desire to be a
homeowner. Although to this day I find the idea of gardening wonderfully
romantic, and love the smell of warm earth, I have absolutely no desire to
actually place my hands *in* dirt; which is to say that a townhome would meet
my needs beautifully.

The first open house I walked into that day was also my last. It only took a
moment to see that it wasn't the right place for me. However, the real estate
agent was a lovely woman; sophisticated yet warm, low-key and focused. I
liked the way she made direct eye contact. Her name, Kricket, was
unassuming and memorable. I was instantly comfortable working with her.
Within moments I found myself telling her about my needs and preferences.

"I think I might have something. I can pull it up on the computer, and if you're interested, we'll schedule a showing."

Kricket worked the keyboard of her laptop. "Now it's not brand new," she warned as the photos loaded, "but I've seen this one, and it is amazingly well-preserved. It sits on the edge of a wetlands. If you like that sort of thing, it's really quite wonderful."

And there it was—I couldn't believe it. The photos were of the model home I had looked at in 1981 with my fiancé. I was instantly flooded with judgment about myself. It went a little like this:

*Oh my gosh! I still love the floor plan! What? Really? Are you saying your tastes haven't changed in 23 years? Oh! I remember how the living room flows up to a writing loft—Now, do you really like it, or are you charmed because you remember the way you felt at 25 when you were in love and excited about the prospect of marriage and a new home? Is this nostalgia sweeping you off your feet? You have had this idea in your head for all of two hours. Don't waste her time. You'll never do this. The last thing you need is to live in a home that will constantly remind you of a failed marriage...*

Really, so much self-judgment is tiring. A month later, I moved into the townhome. I couldn't know that living here in this peaceful, regenerative setting would play such an important role in my spiritual awakening. There are at least six walking paths just outside my door, and never a shortage of wildlife.

When I first moved in, my two cats were especially attracted to the writing loft, and frequently lounged there almost as if they were waiting for me to start writing again. But, lately, it was as if they were disturbed by something. They would lay across my lap or post themselves at my feet and stare up into the loft for long periods of time as if they could see something I couldn't.

Now, did I really believe that something was going on in my loft? I didn't know what to believe. I was learning to accept the truth about life in other dimensions; about spiritual beings who are not "in body." Science tells us that energy is energy. It never goes away; it simply changes form.

As I began to explain the strange reactions of my cats to Trish, she looked past my left ear and nodded. "You have a three-level home?" she asked.

"Yes."

"Your writing loft is at the top of the stairs, and the bedrooms are beyond?"

"You can *see it*?" I asked.

"Yes. Here's what they're showing me," she explained. Her voice was calm, as always. "An earthbound spirit moves between your home and the home next to you. He had trouble with substance abuse and hangs out in your loft and sometimes your kitchen for a contact high."

If someone had taken my photo just then, it would have revealed nothing short of shock and not a little fear. I did not like hearing about a ghost in my home.

"He's been around about 75 years and is not harmful to you but here's the problem. He doesn't like cats. So, he is picking on your cats, especially Tasha."

"Picks on them?"

"Yes, in fact, he lifts up Tasha's tail and pokes at the tender area of her little butt,"

"Does he do this to Talle, too?" I asked.

"Yes, but less so because she's not as excitable. So it's not as fun for him."

This information snapped me from fearful to angry. My cat Tasha is the most gentle animal I've ever met. Entirely black with emerald eyes and a softly whirring purr, she is shy and hides when other people are around. She is a young soul, and fearful of almost everything. It has taken her a long time to trust me, and to find the 'nook' in my lap.

Trish used her arms to make a wide arcing motion then drew both hands to her heart. "Rebecca," she said my name as if it were a caress, "you are so loved. *Killer* is with you, but he prefers to be called *Guardian*, now."

I began to cry. Killer was my twenty-one year-old cat who died in early 2002.

54

"Why is Killer—*Guardian* with me?" I asked Trish. It seemed incredulous.

"We'll come back to that in a minute," Trish said. "Let's deal with your earthbound spirits, first. So, while this earthbound spirit is not intentionally harmful to you, his heaviness and lack of clarity is weighing you down. And, there is a second earthbound spirit, a little girl. She's terribly, terribly sad. Her sadness is also weighing you down."

"There are two things we can do," she continued. "We can for sure make them go away. They do not belong in your space and we can make that clear. We can also offer to help them cross over; to go into the light." Judging from the tone of her voice, this was so commonplace for Trish, we might as well have been talking about the weather.

Okay, I thought trying to catch up, let's recap. Two ghosts—both sad. One old, one young. Both lost. One terrorizes my cats. They make my heart heavy—"I want them gone," I heard myself say, "and I'd like them to go into the light; to cross over."

"We can't *make* them cross over," Trish clarified. We can invite them into the light. We can help them understand that the light is where they're intended to go, and that wonderful things await them. But they have to choose it. If they choose not to go, we will respectfully tell them they do not belong in your space, and they must leave. They are not welcome."

"Okay," I agreed. "What do we do?"

"We're doing it," she said.

Doing what? I wondered. I looked around and couldn't see anything except Trish who was sitting in an erect position, eyes half-closed.

She began to narrate. "I'm telling him he doesn't belong in your home. He seems confused. I'm showing him the light. He won't look in that direction."

"Can *you* see the light?" I asked.

"Yes," she said. Sometimes it's a different color depending on the soul. This light is golden. I'm showing him the light. I've just told him that there are many people who love him on the other side of that light. He's telling me he's never seen the light before. He wants to go but is unsure—oh! There he goes!"

"He went into the light?!"

"Yes," she confirmed. "I'm trying to get the little girl's attention now, but she won't look at me. She won't talk to me but she's walking toward the light. Alright," Trish said, sounding as calm as if she'd just made the bed, or filled the gas tank, or closed a refrigerator door. "She has gone into the light as well."

"They're gone?" I was catching up again.

"Yes, they both went into the light. But there is a lot of stale energy in your loft," she explained. "So, you need to go buy some bells and hang them in your loft. Ring them and dance around the loft to clear out the stale energy and raise the vibration level—revitalize that area!"

Dance!?! She wanted me to dance??!! I am not a dancer!

"Yes," Trish reiterated, and I knew the guides were telling on me again because I had not said this out loud. "You're joyfully taking back your space! Alright," Trish said signaling a change in topic. "They're telling me it's time to help you understand about Guardian."

### Killer 1981-2002
Two months after my mother died, I announced I was getting a cat. I knew my husband didn't want a cat, but that information really didn't seem important to me (you start to get the idea why this marriage didn't work out). So, on Thanksgiving weekend, 1981, I went cat shopping and brought home a tiny six-week old black and white male cat. On the drive home I named him *Killer*, because he crawled up my arm until he found the incurve between my throat and collar bone, and fell asleep, purring softly. He stole my heart.

When I presented Killer to my husband, I set the kitten down on the carpet. He was all of eight inches long, and began to prance around, dainty and elegant, clumsy yet proud. My husband's face melted just as I had suspected because really, who can resist a kitten? If I had understood about energy in those moments, I would have said that my husband's energy immediately changed from resistant and resentful, to open; even welcoming. It rushed forward eagerly to meet this sweet little kitten-being, charmed and delighted. I could almost hear his thoughts. *This isn't going to be bad after all.*

Sadly, Killer chose that moment to squat and pee. And that was the end of that. My husband's energy slammed rearward in retreat so immediately, he literally swayed, back-stepping out of the room.

Twenty years later as I labored over my doctoral dissertation, Killer began to languish. One night I pulled him into my lap and begged him not to leave me until I finished my PhD. "Just a few more months," I whispered into the pink of his ear. The next day, Killer was noticeably improved and soon after that, seemed his usual (if aging) self.

Two months later, I finished my PhD. One month after finishing my PhD, Killer died. And, three months after that, my other cat, Cabot, died.

Two weeks after Cabot passed, raw from the ache of him and desperate for something furry to hold, I went to the Animal Humane Society where Tasha and I found each other. About a year later Talle, my giant calico whose purr clatters like a rusty outboard motor joined our family. She is a sturdy cat. Everything about her is solid. She purrs hard, plays hard, eats hard, and loves hard. Oh, does she love hard! At night when I sleep, she guards me like a dog. And she is a tough task-mistress. She will not let me rest when there is writing to be done.

But, I'm getting ahead of myself again.

ৡৡৡৡ

"When he passed," she explained, "he chose to remain with you to help you open your heart to others. He loves you, and is also helping Tasha, who is a very young soul. Oh, look!" she said, as if I could see what she was seeing. "He's showing me the way he takes Tasha's face between his paws and helps her feel safe and focused. He tells her that it's safe for her to love you."

"Is he a ghost?" I'm always trying to catch up.

"No, he crossed over, but has chosen to remain with you," she repeated. "He wants you to know that his passing was peaceful. It involved a lot of gentle stroking and loving. "

I was crying hard now, remembering the trauma of Killer's passing. As Killer's body began to fail him, I didn't understand what was happening. For two days, Killer kept dragging his body to the darkest corner he could find. He had stopped eating or drinking. He could no longer make his back legs work. Yet, I couldn't let myself believe he was dying. Each time I found him in a dark corner, I would carry him into the light or lay him gently by his food.

Finally, he crawled to the back of the linen closet. There was a rotting smell about him and I knew he was in agony. The only thing to do was to have him put down. It was late on a Sunday afternoon. Veterinary clinics were closed. My friend Joyce helped me rush Killer to the Animal Humane Society. We arrived about five minutes before closing time. I was weeping loudly holding Killer so close I don't know how he could breathe, all the while pleading, "don't leave me, please don't leave me."

I became even more distraught when they told me I could not be in the room with him when they put him down. The thought of Killer meeting death at the hands of a stranger was beyond bearable, but they were firm, and I couldn't stand for him to suffer another moment.

They carried him away in a wire-frame basket. I remember thinking how cold and uncomfortable it looked. As the distance widened between us, Killer suddenly sat up and looked back at me. To me, it seemed as if he was trying to leap out of the basket. I heard him yelp, and then he disappeared through the stainless steel doors that displayed the warning, 'no admittance'.

But I didn't have to tell a word of this to Trish. She already knew. "He wants you to know that his soul left his body just before he disappeared through those doors. The yelp you heard, was joyful. He was joyful to be released from the pain of his body. He is an old soul," she smiled. "Very dignified."

Then she leaned forward and released two drops of essential oil, frankincense and something else, into my open palm.

"What is this for?" I asked.

"To help you hear what they're going to share with you next."

I waited in wonder.

"Guardian came through today to help you understand one of the most important truths of the universe." She paused before continuing. "You are never alone— none of us is ever alone. A multitude of souls support us in our earthly lives. During our sessions together you've begun to open yourself to new spiritual truths. You've learned you have guides, your mother is with you, even the soul of your cat is with you. And, he's working with Tasha to help her be a good pet partner. And it doesn't stop there."

"A multitude of souls support you," she repeated. "So, while you are struggling with the enormity of overcoming depression and creating a new professional role, you are endlessly supported by the love of countless souls."

We sat with that in silence for awhile. Finally Trish said, "We are complete."

But I wasn't quite done. "Sometimes I worry that Talle feels a little like the red-headed step-child because Tasha needs so much attention."

Trish smiled, "Talle, is an older soul and very independent. She's glad Guardian is working with Tasha. Most importantly, she wants you to know that she is your writing inspiration."

So I *will* write again?" I asked.

"You will have the *choice* to write again," Trish answered.

*"... dance is the hidden language of the soul."*
— Martha Graham (1894-1991)

# *Unity*

**December 6, 2006**

Linda and I met for lunch, ordered chicken Caesar salads, and I began to pitch my ideas about the position she had suggested earlier that week. I was nervous and frustrated with myself because I am generally engagingly articulate, yet my words kept sticking, and my manner was dogged.

The problem was simple. While I believed in the position I was presenting to Linda, I didn't think I was the best candidate. I wasn't being humble. The position was an okay fit; just not a great fit. Was it really too much, I wondered, to find a great fit?

But, it was already December. Time was running short.

Linda listened intently and with enthusiasm, nodding and occasionally tossing in a few ideas of her own. After awhile I realized this was not a pitch at all. We were actually creating something together. The tightness in my chest eased and the exchange of ideas came more easily.

It was in this considerably more relaxed state that I felt a dome of warm, golden light settle over me. The light brought clarity. My guides were helping me! I didn't have to know everything. They were teaching me that this was the magic of letting someone else in; a natural act of co-creation.

In the next moment, I was given two views of the world, as if there was a second me floating overhead watching as Linda and I chatted. The floating me actually saw our two souls meet in the middle of the table and form one soul, even though our physical bodies never changed attitude. *This is what an out-of-body experience is*, I realized. This is what unity feels like.

"I'll work on getting this to the right people," Linda assured me. "Your job is to continue mapping it out and be ready to take it to the next level. I'll get back to you."

*"...what I give form to in daylight is only one percent of what I have seen in darkness."*

—M.C. Escher (1898-1972)

# *Wet Death*

**Session Five of Six — December 12, 2006**
Six days later I was sitting in my fifth session with Trish in silent hysteria. I couldn't stop crying. I couldn't talk. I couldn't explain the endless tears.

"How did lunch with Linda go?" Trish asked.

I shrugged. It was an inelegant shrug. A sort of *why are you asking me to explain something that can't be explained* kind of shrug you might expect from a sixteen-year-old. It wasn't that I didn't want to explain, it was that I simply couldn't find the energy.

"They're telling me it went well," Trish prompted.

I shrugged again.

"How did you leave things?" she asked.

I started to cry harder. "She was going to get back to me, but I haven't heard from her."

And that was the problem. I hadn't heard from her. My intuition told me our proposal had been rejected. I was pretty sure that meant she didn't know yet, what to do next, and so she hadn't gotten back to me. Although I knew it to be unreasonable, I felt abandoned. One minute we were building something together, the next she disappeared.
"Abandonment is one of the lessons you're learning in this lifetime." Everything about Trish in that moment was gentle, soft, wise. "Do you really

think she has abandoned you?"

"No—she just doesn't know what to do next. She's so influential, she's not used to having her pitches reje—" I trailed off, unable to finish my sentence.

The weather had turned wintry dark. Trish lit a tea light and placed it inside a white crystal holder. The flame caught at the crystal and began to glow.

"See how the light alone is a small flame at the end of a wick," she said. "But when the light is placed inside the crystal holder, it glows brightly and is all at once beautiful, inspirational and peaceful. You are like the flame inside the crystal, Rebecca. This is what it is to be human. Your light has been placed in an earthly body."

We were quiet. More silent tears streamed down my face and dropped onto my lap.

"This feels like wet death," I finally said. "It's as if something in me is dying."

"Yes," she agreed. "You are letting go of what doesn't serve you well anymore so that your light can shine more brightly. You are recommitting to your earthly life. It requires you to feel. As you let those feelings in, your higher consciousness and your earthly self are integrating."

We were quiet again.

After several moments Trish released essential oils into the air and then said, "Your guides have called for reinforcements. They've asked for all the healers to join them, and they are circling around you in clockwise motion. They represent amaranthine love. Their purpose is to heal you."

The image was so pure, it made me cry even harder.

"We all break, Rebecca. And their message is that we are all healable. You are healable. Your light is growing brighter with every tear."

*Amaranthine Love Acknowledged*
Artist: Phyllis E. Smith

*"...one cannot find peace in work or in pleasure, in the world or in*
*a convent, but only in one's soul."*
— W. Somerset Maugham (1874-1965)

# *Peace*

## Session Six of Six — December 27, 2006

Two weeks later, I stood outside Trish's door enjoying the feel of the distant Minnesota sun on my face. I love winter. I always have. Snow removal and driving icy roads won't win any awards with me but I love the way the air bites, the snow cleans, and half the mammal world sleeps.

As I was preparing to leave my previous session with Trish two weeks earlier, she suggested I do a soul visit with Linda.

"A soul visit," she explained, is a way to connect your higher consciousness with that of someone else. A lot can be accomplished in a soul visit because it shortens the distance between people."

Before going to sleep, I was to lie in bed and visualize my soul projecting out of my head. Once I had this image, I was to call to Linda's soul and ask to chat. Then, I was to imagine the two of us in the sky. I might even feel her arrive.

"It's fine if you don't feel anything," Trish assured me. "The soul visit will happen because you asked for it, even if you don't feel it happening."

That same night I attempted the soul visit. I did not feel Linda 'arrive' and fell asleep almost immediately. But I believed that the soul visit would happen because I *intended* for it to happen, and that it would make a difference.

The next morning I left the warmth of my bed and headed downstairs feeling extraordinarily refreshed. I dropped a handful of coffee beans into the grinder, and then experienced a strange sensation, almost as if I'd been nudged.

*Why was I being nudged* I wondered. *Who was nudging me?*

With no additional data available, I shrugged it off and tapped the coarsely ground beans into the filter. Just as I pressed 'brew', an idea for a new position popped. A soft effervescence swept over me as I realized just how much the idea excited me!

Although it was early morning, I didn't hesitate. I booted up my computer mentally writing a new job proposal to share with Linda. When my email finally opened (a mere, yet eternal three minutes later) I couldn't believe it. An email from Linda was already waiting for me. It said 'call me!' So I did, and we immediately began to work on our ideas for this new position.

It was a winner! *I* was a winner! The outcome was a promotion, a completely new focus, and an opportunity to utilize more of my doctoral expertise.

I was a Phoenix, rising from the ashes!

ৡৡৡৡ

When I was a little girl my mother dutifully read fairy tales to us because we loved them. When we were old enough, she made it clear that she thought they were silly. She still read them to us, but there were times when she couldn't hold back a disgusted snort. One of my favorites was *The Snow Queen* by Hans Christian Andersen. For those who do not know the story, two children, Gerda and Kay, are playing when Kay unwittingly offends the snow queen, who places splinters of ice in Kay's eye and heart. He instantly grows as cold and remote as the snow queen, and remains so until Gerda's warm embrace melts the ice.

Even though it was a wintry day, I was smiling because most of my fear had been released, and like Kay, my heart was melted. I had a new job, a new future, a few more days of vacation, and as soon as the door opened I'd be in another session with Trish learning more about life and light. I could feel my guides rolling with glee. They made me giggle.

ৡৡৡৡ

Always present at each of my sessions with Trish, my mother generally took a back seat to my guides. At appropriate times she would come forward to reinforce their counsel, and to remind me of her love. In this sixth and last session she kept showing Trish the image of wild horses pulling a carriage. The first time she did this, Trish asked her what the significance of the image was. My mother smiled, and then tossed wide the reins, allowing the horses to run free.

"Oh, I get it," Trish said, "Your mother is saying, 'throw wide the reins, Rebecca'. She's telling you it's time to let go, now. You worked together with others to create an enormous professional change in eight weeks, and now it's time to enjoy what you've accomplished. Just let the rest of the pieces fall naturally into place. Feel the relief. *Throw wide the reins.*"

My mother is so cool.

By releasing control, I would allow possibilities to present themselves and give nurturance to my intuition.

My guides came forward laughing, applauding and skipping. When Trish asked why they were skipping they told her I had a skip in my step, now. They suggested visualizing a skip in my step as a tool for me to use to link to joy. The moment Trish shared this with me, I felt more light-hearted and actually saw myself skipping.

"They're giving you this tool because you asked to feel joy," Trish told me. Amazing. I had not shared this with her.

During this session my guides also told me that my empath was going to have a large role in my next professional adventure, and that I needed to remember to live in my heart, instead of my head. I would have a lot of questions for my guides in the near future, and I should remember to ask them from my heart—if I ask them from my head, they will not answer me because now I know the difference. Intuition is the portal from head to heart.

"The brain spins," Trish said. "The heart knows what to do with it." To strengthen my intuition, I had to keep working on thinking from my heart.

A few days later I was shopping and overheard a woman say, "the brain is just a computer. It needs the heart to fuel it." I have no idea who she was or in what context she was using that statement, but it has helped me remember to think from my heart, more often.

"Rebecca, a new energy has joined us," Trish announced.

By now statements like this were less startling. "Who?" I asked.

"Nelson Mandela."

"But he's not dead—hasn't passed, has he?" I queried.

"Souls do not have to be passed to come together in support," she explained. "Before you came into this world, you made agreements with scores of souls to support you along the way. Some of them chose to live human lives at the same time as you, but that doesn't limit them from supporting you."

"So, Nelson Mandela is a supporter of mine?

"He's more of a teacher for you. Our souls join with other souls both in the ether and here on earth, even when we're awake. It has to do with quantum physics. Time and place are really concepts we've created to suit us, but the truth is, we're everywhere all the time."

Quantum physics was not a new concept for me; I had studied it a little when I was working on my doctorate. But I had never thought of it in terms of souls coming together to support one another.

"As you move into this next professional role," she continued, "you're moving deeper into the work you chose for yourself before coming into this life. So Nelson Mandela's energy has joined us to give you a new tool. He is raising his arm, fist closed, and is telling the 'unite story'. Do you know this story?"

I didn't.

"It's actually a technique he uses. Nelson Mandela appeared in public, soon after being freed. The crowd was largely all black. It was an angry assemblage. When Mandela began to speak, he raised his arm and clenched his fist shouting, 'Black Power'. After every few sentences, he repeated this action. Each time he did this, the crowd raised their fists in support and roared 'Black Power'.

As Mandela continued to speak and punch his phrases with raised fist shouting 'Black power' the crowd responded in kind. Then, after awhile, Mandela raised his fist and changed his words slightly to 'Blacks Unite' and the crowd roared appreciatively 'Blacks Unite'.

Finally Mandela raised his fist and shouted, 'ALL UNITE' and the crowd roared 'ALL UNITE'. In that moment, the malevolent energy of the crowd began to dissipate.

"This is Mandela's method of taking people up a level at a time," Trish interpreted, "and is a great example of entrainment. His message to you, Rebecca, is to remember to take people up a level at a time. It's all about meeting people where they are, and helping them move forward. You might begin by silently asking, 'at what level do we need to travel together' each time you meet someone. This begins the flow of spiritual energy between you and the other person. Your guides will help you understand at what level you are to begin."

In the next moment, my mother and Nelson Mandela, along with a new presence, the soul of Mahatma Gandhi, came forward. Together, the three of them made the motion of 'throwing wide the reins'.

So often we believe that in order to entrain others to us, we have to control the situation. But my mother, Mandela and Gandhi indicated the opposite. The art of entrainment is not about control. It's about working with the other person's energy. It's about asking 'at what level do we need to travel together' and entrainment becomes organic.

Throughout this session the message came through repeatedly that my new position would open a new world to me. What a promising professional future the universe and I had created together! I was grateful to God, to my guides, to Trish, my mother, Guardian, my ascended masters, the angels, my former manager, Linda, my new manager, and all who helped me with this transition.

I also fully appreciated my own contribution to this wonderful outcome. How different I was from the shame-filled, harshly self-critical, frightened woman who was encased in mind-numbing depression and paralyzed by self-doubt.

I was filled with light and living brave!

*"...healing is a matter of time, but it is sometimes also a matter of opportunity."*

— Hippocrates

# *Gathering*

**May-June, 2007**
So, here I was in a new place in my life, learning to look at the world through a new lens, with soft eyes. In the Japanese art of Aikido, the practice of 'soft eyes' means to widen one's periphery to take in more of the world, with less judgment. The idea is that it's easier to maintain calm when we are not over-focused. When we are not over-focused, we are less judgmental and are able to feel and return love more fully and freely.

A few weeks into my new position I realized just how important it was to continue my spiritual growth, and I began meeting with Trish on a regular basis. Some of my greatest focus was learning to remind myself that 'they will answer if you ask'. Over and over the message had been 'just ask us, Rebecca. We'll tell you'. But this was a very difficult concept for me to hold on to. Ask someone? Be guided? Trust someone else? I had always depended on *my* brain and *my* intuition.

**May, 2007**
In early spring Trish invited me into a four-week group session. I was hesitant, preferring to grow alone, and then recognized the flaw in my thought process. Spiritual growth is all about connection; with God, with our own higher consciousness, and with others, both in human form and those who are not in body. By this time I had learned to 'hear' my guides at least some of the time, and their counsel was clear—it was time to learn with others.

In our first session we were asked to introduce ourselves by bringing a song or photo, artwork, a poem; something that represented who we were and what was important in our lives. I put this exercise off to the last minute for reasons I didn't fully understand. Then, the night before our first meeting, I found myself reaching for one of the many volumes of poetry in my library; an anthology with poets such as Anne Sexton, Galway Kinnel, Mary Oliver, Denise Levertov, and let the book fall open where it would. I was captivated by Henry Taylor's *Riding Lesson,* a metaphor about learning lessons and managing life.

Next, I encountered Wendell Berry's *The Vacation* about a man who was so busy filming his vacation he was quite literally on the outside looking in. This poem startled me; then haunted me. It spoke to me on an intimate, almost cellular level about how important it is to be fully ourselves and fully in our lives.

Poem after poem struck me when finally I realized that my guides were taking me on a personalized tour, reintroducing me to this world of image-through-word. Infused with poetry, I had fistfuls of poems and no idea how to narrow it to just one.

About mid-way through our first session Trish asked us to share why we were participating in this group. I listened to each participant and wondered what I would say. When it was my turn, I heard a small voice say, "I want to love myself into being." *I* had said that—*me*.

When I realized it was my voice, I knew I had discovered my most basic truth. I began to cry. And for the first time my tears held no shame, no feelings of inadequacy or the dreadful knowledge that I was a diurnal disappointment to myself or someone else. They were evidence of discovering the purest form of love and desire; love of self, and desire for self-wholeness. I had reached the calyx of healing.

## Calyx

Long
have I slept
  a bud
Waiting
for the Light to
  unfurl my
soul

The homework for our second session was to create something that represented our individual uniqueness. Inspired by the poetry I'd found, I was ready to get creative. Yet no project came to mind. A few days later, I was wandering through Michael's with a friend when clear as day, my guides said 'birdhouse' and led me to the aisle where I could choose from any number of birdhouse kits.

Intrigued, I followed this rather alien instinct and spent my weekend working on a birdhouse—an entirely new experience! While I thoroughly enjoyed myself, when I was done it was clear that this was not the project 'they' had in mind. Crossly, I pushed the birdhouse aside muttering something like, "then why did you tell me to do this?" and went for a walk.

There is a line in Lawrence Raab's poem, *My Life Before I Knew It* that reads, "One day, one of those strangers would introduce herself to me, and then the life I'd never been able to foresee would begin, and everything before I became myself would appear necessary to the rest of the story." During my walk it came to me that my guides were telling me to 'go and write a poem about the birdhouse you created'. Realization began to dawn. Somehow, creating the birdhouse was necessary to the true project, which was to write a poem.

But I hadn't written in ten years. If I could translate communication with my guides into words—which is nearly impossible to do—we simply don't have language that is adequate—the flash of instant knowing they gave me plays out something like this:

Me: How can you expect me to just sit down and write a poem? Note: I'm actually feeling indignant that they're telling me it's time to do something I desperately want to do again.

Guides: You've never created a birdhouse before.

Me: Meaning? (I was deliberately being stubborn.)

Guides: Writing a poem feels impossible to you; as if you'd never done it before. Well, you never created a birdhouse before, but look at it. It's remarkable.
Me: It's *not* remarkable.

Guides: The point is, you're in a highly creative state and if you can create a birdhouse, you can create a poem. It's time, Rebecca.

It really was as simple as that. I sat down to write and although it didn't just pop out, there was indeed a poem waiting to be written. Originally named 'Birdhouse' I later changed it to 'Small Places'.

## Small Places

The wise woman says sometimes
you come to me
as a bird
So I built you a birdhouse.

Centuries ago
you taught me to sing
You, with your throaty smudge
leaving the higher notes to me
like thick, dark coffee and sweet cream
Where grit and the sublime collide.

But in this life you are spirit
You come to me
as a bird
So I built you a birdhouse

Even though my heart knows
none of us is meant to hide
in small places

Within a couple of weeks I'd written two other poems. It felt miraculous. I kept saying to myself, "I can't believe that I am actually writing again." And then suddenly I dried up and couldn't write. It was as if after three poems, everything felt trite, overused, boring.

I would learn later that I had shut down my ability to write because I was in a state of disbelief. I literally made it go away because instead of thanking God for the return of this divine gift, I kept voicing my disbelief. This is simple, basic physics—the law of attraction. Our energy attracts what we are most focused on. I was focused on disbelief until I could no longer write—because I believed myself incapable of writing, I became incapable of writing.

*"...there are two ways to live; we can live as if nothing is a miracle; we can live as if everything is a miracle."*

— Albert Einstein

## *Flying Lessons*

**June, 2007**
Trish and I had begun discussions about animal totems. To embrace the spirituality of animal totems, we need to embrace the belief that we are one with nature. Our spiritual connectedness to nature allows us to experience a symbiosis with animals, depending on our individual needs, which change as we change. Animal totems express the spirit nature of its species and exemplify qualities from which we can learn. In this way, animal totems are spiritual tools; archetypes that work with the subconscious mind tapping into the energy that is present in all things. Like frequencies of a radio, totems come to us depending on our individual needs.

The wetlands that spring were vibrant with wildlife. Mornings I would awaken and hear the ducks splashing in the pond, calling to one another. Watching their water-play, I felt the joy I'd been asking for burble up. Birds flocked to the half a dozen bird feeders on my deck, and drew long drinks from the bird bath. Red wing blackbirds that nest in the grassier area of the wetlands visited regularly, along with chickadees, gold finches, nuthatches, cardinals, blue jays, orioles, and more woodpeckers than I'd ever seen in my life. One of the red oaks just outside my window was a haven for them.

"Why so many birds?" I asked Trish. "This is my third summer here and I've never seen this many birds before."

"They are teaching you to fly, Rebecca. They are teaching you how to use your physical body to understand your intuition. Your body is your best psychic tool. Honor it."

I loved the metaphor of 'learning to fly' but did not understand what she meant about my body being a tool for my intuition.

"How are you like a bird?" she asked me. When I didn't know, she said, "That is something for you to meditate about."

In June, I began preparations to facilitate a particularly challenging three-day business retreat, when a new bird arrived at the bird feeder. A lot was dependent on the successful outcome of this retreat. The greatest challenge would be to help a highly intellectual group of individuals move from their heads to their hearts, where they could begin to function more as a team, fully invested in the success of one another.

The new bird was about the size of a gold finch, and was an astoundingly brilliant turquoise with a beak as yellow as a banana. It looked like an indigo bunting, but the yellow beak was wrong. As the calendar drew nearer to the three-day retreat, three more brilliant turquoise birds with yellow beaks came to my feeders. I was intrigued. So, I searched the Internet to try to learn more. In every case I found that the indigo bunting has a black beak. Apparently, there was no such thing as an indigo bunting with a yellow beak. In fact, it appears there is no such bird as an all blue bird with a yellow beak.

I also looked for information about indigo bunting totems and found only that the indigo bird, such as the indigo bunting speaks of knowledge and intelligence. Then, just as I was about to give up, I found the following conversation on one of the bird guide blogs:

> **Question** - Blue bird with yellow beak:
> I live in western Iowa near Omaha, Nebraska. This evening I saw a royal blue bird with a yellow beak at the finch feeder with the goldfinches. It was the same size as the finches and it acted like a finch. I see that other people are asking about this bird also. I don't think it's an indigo bunting because of the beak. We've had our feeder up for 5 years and this is the first one we've seen.
> **Answer**: I'd almost bet my last dollar on this one. Soooo many people think that the Indigo Buntings have a yellow beak, and in certain lighting conditions it can appear that way. Does this help convince you?
>
> **Response**: I saw my bird at my feeder, 10 feet away, both upper and lower parts of beak were banana yellow. Crystal.

**Answer**: Nobody has been able to photo-document claims of an all blue bird with a yellow bill. No photos have been posted that show a yellow bill. All photos of Indigo Bunting show a shiny dark bill. There is no living bird that fits the description of an all blue bird with a yellow bill. European Starling has a yellow bill and some shiny blue coloration. Indigo Bunting is all blue but never has a yellow bill. Take your choice, but there is no other answer.

After I returned from my challenging three-day retreat exultant about how successful it was, I noticed the turquoise birds were gone. All of the other birds, as well as dozens of woodpeckers, remained. From that time to this, the startling turquoise birds with yellow beaks have never returned.

Were those birds—birds that have never been documented—totems? Did they come to lend support and inspiration?

I learned later that birds are the communicators of the animal kingdom and can communicate across all species. They warn, teach and convey messages from one animal to another. The birds, I realized were not just teaching me to fly—they were reminding me of how important it was that I find my voice.

*"...smells of nature are invisible, so they take your mind to the invisible realm of spirit, where things vibrate higher and faster than matter. There are healing properties in nature. Also, there are very real nature angels. You can ask these nature angels to heal you. Being in nature helps you to adapt to the natural rhythm of the earth, and since timing and cycles are a part of everything, you become more in sync with the rhythm of life. Air, sunshine, and fragrance of flowers all help you to meditate at deeper levels. Venture outside and ask the nature angels to surround you."*

— Global Oneness

## *Rhythm*

**July-August, 2007**

In subsequent sessions, I learned that between earthly lives, we do many things, and sometimes we simply need to heal. I once heard Echo Bodine describe it as a time where those souls who need it simply rest, levitating in the sun just above softly waving grass where they feel only love. Nothing is expected of them except to be loved into wholeness again. Other times we are ready to help other souls.

I could feel my mother closer than ever, now, and was so grateful that she was a soul who, if she had needed intensive healing following her lifetime as my mother, had completed that process and was present in my life, now. Sometimes I could discern my mother's messages from the messages of my guides. All communication from this spiritual realm is based in boundless love. There is no judgment. Our guides do not lecture, they don't scold. They do at times find loving ways to remind me that I already know something, but all messages are loving. Some messages may contain guidance about what to do next. Some messages may be more urgent than others. But they are always born out of love, and a commitment to helping us fulfill our purpose.

Because all messages are so loving, it is not always easy to ascertain who is 'talking' to me. Often I know. As often, I don't know. Trish has promised that one day I will be able to tell because a certain area of my body will signal "mom" or "guides" or even "Archangel Michael" and so forth. So, although I could not always tell whether it was my mother or my guides, I could feel her more closely than ever before.

Meanwhile, the woodpeckers on my deck increased and I marveled at what a beautiful bird they are, and how I'd never seen so many of them. Every once in awhile Trish would tell me, "your mother sometimes comes to you as a bird." At times, Trish would read my poem "Small Places" out loud to me.

Till finally one day I asked the question they were all waiting for me to ask, "Does my mother come to me as the same bird? If so, what kind of bird?"

Trish smiled and said, "that is for you to discover. She is suggesting you go out on your deck and ask her to reveal herself to you."

But I didn't do it. Something in the back of my mind kept saying over and over, 'what if I do it and she doesn't answer?'

So I asked Trish this question in a subsequent session and she replied, "Then ask again. Be sure you are asking from your heart, not your head. She won't answer you if you're asking from your head."

I wasn't clear about what this meant. I'd heard it before and could never quite hold on to the impression I was given. Later, I came to realize that when we ask things for the purpose of proving something, we're not asking from our heart because the heart doesn't need proof. It is the mind that needs proof. The heart simply knows. If I was asking my mother to prove that she comes to me as a bird, she would not answer.

One morning in August about a month after this conversation, I felt compelled to ask. It was almost as if I could hear my guides chanting, 'you're ready, you're ready, you're ready'. I stepped out on the deck and listened to the chatter and buzz of the wetlands. I saw a turtle sunning on a log. Squirrels and chipmunks scurried off and disappeared. The ducks were at the far end of the pond, swimming quietly. Silently. That's when I began to realize that in the few moments I'd been out on the deck, the entire wetlands had quieted to a hush. The only birds I could see were blue jays.

I raised my arms up and gave thanks for my life, for the earth, for the wetlands. And then I asked God and my guides to help me be in my heart. I was quiet then, waiting to feel the steady rhythm of my heartbeat.

"Sometimes you come to me as a bird," I whispered. "Come to me now. Show yourself."

I want to step back from this story a moment and comment about how frightened I was to do this. All along, I'd sort of kept one foot safely rooted in my former belief system, whatever that was, ready to jump out and say something like 'this was just an exploration—I never really believed it...' in case it turned out to be a farce. By asking my mother to reveal herself to me, I was making the choice to pull that foot out of the safety zone; to commit myself to this new spirituality in full. I knew if I didn't, she wouldn't answer me. If I was not fully committed, then I would be asking her to prove herself to me. But if I committed, I would be asking from my heart for the purpose of feeling her love more fully.

So there I was out on the deck aware that I had fully crossed over. And I had just asked my mother to show herself. The wetlands grew even more silent. I couldn't see a bird anywhere. I waited for an unknown amount of time while even the wind quieted. But she did not come.

I asked again. Still no birds anywhere. I couldn't imagine how that was happening. There was always an abundance of birds.

The silence was broken suddenly by the screech of a blue jay. I looked up and saw him circling high above the trees. The wind picked up and the blue jay was joined by a dozen other blue jays. They flew high overhead circling and screeching. My heart turned over in disappointment.

"Really?" I asked, wondering if she could possibly be a blue jay. No offense to blue jays but it just didn't seem to fit. It's only fair to note that blue jays are actually very handy totems who help with developing adaptive behaviors, awareness of personal power, higher knowledge, tenacity and resourcefulness. At the time, I was not aware of this and I thought of blue jays as seemingly arrogant.

The blue jays flew out of sight and quiet resettled over the wetlands.

"Really?" I asked again, and as I did, the blue jays returned screeching and squawking like querulous siblings.

I dropped my head feeling oddly disappointed, nearly convinced she was indeed a blue jay, and began to turn away to go inside.

And then, from nowhere it seemed, came a beautiful female downy woodpecker. She flew to the deck rail and landed about two feet from where I stood. She surveyed me solemnly, then hopped a bit closer. My arms broke out in goose-flesh, my third chakra vibrated, and my sixth chakra burned. I could feel the hair on my head straighten at the root.

We stood there, this female downy woodpecker and I. For how long, I honestly don't know. When I finally found my voice I said, "it's you."

She looked at me.

"I know it's you. I knew you couldn't be a blue jay. You've been trying to tell me this for months now. It started when you kept me company on those walks around the lake."

As soon as I said this, I realized it had not begun with the lake walks. In fact, she had been with me for many, many lifetimes. The time she spent with me on those walks around the lake was the beginning of my coming into consciousness about how out-of-body souls connect with us; to teach us new truths, and to feel their love. Bird medicine was just one of her techniques.

"Thank you," I said. I wasn't entirely sure what I was thanking her for. Everything, I guess.

With that, the woodpecker dipped her head as if in a bow, and then flew to the woodpecker tree where she joined with a half a dozen other woodpeckers.

It was several days later when I realized how choreographed that moment was. The blue jays were the natural world's version of *Pomp and Circumstance*. My mother wanted to be sure I would not miss her message. The blue jays joyfully heralded the importance of what was going to happen next. The wetlands fell to a hush, and I achieved a state of 'soft eyes'.

Today, only a few woodpeckers remain. Once I finally crossed over fully into believing she was with me, she didn't need to send scores of woodpeckers to my feeders. From that day to this, she appears on my deck when I am having deeply spiritual conversations with people, and at times, when I am writing. I have never asked her to show herself again because I haven't felt the need to see her; I can feel her all the time. For example right now as I write this, she hovers over my right shoulder and sometimes I hear her whisper, "well done, Rebecca."

There is a wonderful website by Star Stuffs. On it I found the following description about birds: *birds hold the knowledge of speaking with all animals. All feathers relate to human spirit and its innate connection to the Divine. They are the "initiators of air" in opening to realms beyond physical time and space. Psychic perceptions are thus transformed into spiritual intentions. Air separates heaven and earth, thus the birds are the epitome of the flight between spiritual and physical being. With bird medicine, we learn to use our innate intuition to ride the currents of life.*

The woodpecker totem shows us the beat of life; helps us maintain rhythm and teaches us how to balance the spiritual and mental aspects with the physical world for harmony through tenacity and straight-forward actions.

Feeling the beat of life has been instrumental to finding my voice. Although I had not picked up on it, the importance of rhythm was introduced to me in my first session with the intuitive astrologer, Nancy. During that session she was interpreting rapidly for my mother who explained that part of the reason I was having a problem with depression was because as I lost people, instead of letting them go, I would give them a piece of my soul. I needed to reclaim these pieces in order to grow from fractured to whole. One way to do this was to beat a drum and ask for my soul to return to wholeness. I was to ask for, and then visualize my soul as whole; complete.

This is an example of inadequate language. I understood the *words* Nancy said, but I simply didn't have enough *context*, and lost this information almost as soon as it was shared with me. Later, during our group sessions, Trish brought out a drum she had made under the guidance of one of her mentors. She talked about the beat of life and importance of drumming. Drumming can help us achieve a symbiosis between our human existence and the desires of our soul. This is what my mother was trying to help me understand, and why she sometimes comes to me as a beautiful woodpecker. That, and the fact that love never dies; it never goes away. It simply changes form.

*"...since love grows within you, so beauty grows. For love is the beauty of the soul."*

—*St. Augustine*

# *Ariana*

**August, 2007**
Very soon after this, I learned my soul's name. I was lying on my sofa about to enjoy a quick nap. In those softly descending moments before sleep the name *Ariana* came to me. It was a breathy melody, full of light. A confection so whisper-sweet, I knew it was the voice of my spiritual guides revealing the true name of my soul. It is the one of the few times I've actually understood my guides through hearing them. Typical communication with them is through impressions that come in quick, brief flashes, and are often difficult to hold on to because there is so much in those flashes.

In recent months I had felt a longing that I didn't fully understand. After they said *Ariana* I was given the powerful impression that my guides were smiling because I had asked to know myself more clearly, and this was their gift. The unnamed longing I had been feeling was the desire to know myself.

It was happening. I was loving myself into being, and as a part of that process, I was beginning to find my voice.

**August 3, 2007**
"Your guides and energies are presenting much more densely," Trish offered.

Just when I think she can't surprise me anymore, she does. 'Presenting much more densely'. Not to be dense, but what does that mean, I wondered?

"I can see your guides and your high vibrational energy with the naked eye. I don't have to go into theta state to see it," she explained, although I had not yet asked.

"Is that because they have become so real to me? I feel them all the time. At times it seems like I'm talking with them all the time. Sometimes I am so bombarded with impressions from them, yet I don't always understand what they're telling me, but *oh boy* are they ever *there*!"

"You listen best through your fingers," she answered. "They are your channel."

I knew she was suggesting I would achieve greater clarity by returning to my writing, but I just couldn't get there.

When I told Trish about hearing the name *Ariana*, she smiled and said, "How did your body feel when you heard it?"

"Everything tingled. It was a little like the afterglow of an orgasm, if you know what I mean," I said, feeling just a little embarrassed.

"Exactly!" Trish agreed. "And that's how you can tell whether the message is being divinely communicated, or whether you're just guessing. Your body is your best tool for understanding divine messages."

She'd said this to me many times, but this was the first time I actually understood what she meant.

"In fact," Trish said, you have a habit of placing your left hand over the soft enclave between your shoulder and your breast, near your heart. Do you know why you do that?"

I shook my head. I didn't even know I had that mannerism.

"Because that's where your higher consciousness rests. She says 'hello' by the way."

"Is this where everyone's higher consciousness is?" I asked.

"It's different for different people," she answered. "One way to get in touch with her is to hold your hand over your heart. You can access answers, summon courage, accomplish solidarity—just a light touch to your heart or shoulder."

*"...if you want to write you must have faith in yourself. Faith enough to believe that if a thing is true about you, it is likely true about many people. And if you can have faith in your integrity and your motives, then you can write without fear."*

— anonymous author of Real Live Preacher

# *Bending Time*

## August – September, 2007

In late August, I was compelled by my guides to pull together all the remnants of my poetry. Through various impressions they said, "It's time to gather together your poetry, Rebecca."

But I didn't feel ready. I couldn't name what was stopping me exactly; only that I felt highly resistant to begin the process. So, I ignored their urgings.

They were persistent and reminded me repeatedly that I didn't have all my poetry in one place, or even one medium. Some of it was scribbled on napkins or small pieces of paper. Some of it was on various hard drives, and possibly even old floppy disks. Never mind that I no longer had a computer that would read disks. I was at risk of losing all that I had written. This realization created a vague undercurrent of discontent, but my resistance was stronger than my discontent.

"I really don't care if it's all lost," I muttered out loud one day.

"But I *do* care," came a stronger voice. It was Ariana. And she would not be silenced. I remember thinking how foolish it would be to continue the argument—Ariana had already won because she knew my true heart; my true desire.

It was like stepping into a time warp. I went upstairs to my loft to begin pulling the pieces of my poetry together and came back downstairs three days later. For three days and nights I worked almost non-stop locating, collecting, organizing and cataloging my poetry.

It turned into a love affair.

Some of the poetry was just awful. Some of it was embarrassingly sweet or naive. Some of it was so painful, reading it felt like walking on shards of glass. Some of it was quite wonderful.

There came a point during those three days when I realized I had not intentionally stopped writing creatively. It simply had become necessary in order to focus on completing my master's and PhD. And, during those years of separation, I began to forget. For instance, I forgot about the joy of finding a fresh way to express myself. I forgot about the pungent energy that is both released and captured during the writing process. I had even forgotten my dream that one day, one of my poems would find its way into a textbook or anthology to be discussed at length by serious-minded literature majors.

When I emerged from my three-day journey, I realized that everything I had written or tried to write was all necessary to my evolution. Writing for me is the way I achieve transformation. Evolution and transformation is messy, imperfect, and always a process that involves feelings, expression, and change.

My love for writing and my need to write, is a lot like singing. All my life, I've loved to sing. When I was a young child, I innocently thought I was a great singer. Over time I began to realize this was not the case.

Years later as a young adult I joined my church choir, still wishing I could be a great singer, and knowing I was not. Yet, a wonderful surprise awaited me because I found that I was indeed a great singer; a great *choir* singer, that is. I blend, I watch the director, I follow, I learn music easily, and I love singing in a choir. Today, that's enough. But in my early days when I knew I would never be great, yet still desired to be great, I used to think how cruel it was to have mammoth desire and only mediocre talent.

Through my primary guide, Thomas, it was revealed to me that this is the classic struggle between ego and human spirituality. Our ego, he said desires things like recognition, fame, and success. It causes us to need to be right and can interfere with our ability to forgive. It also helps us maintain a healthy self-esteem, and for this reason, it is very important.

To help me understand this better, Thomas and a host of spiritual beings guided me in the development of the following model for spiritual connectedness and fulfillment.

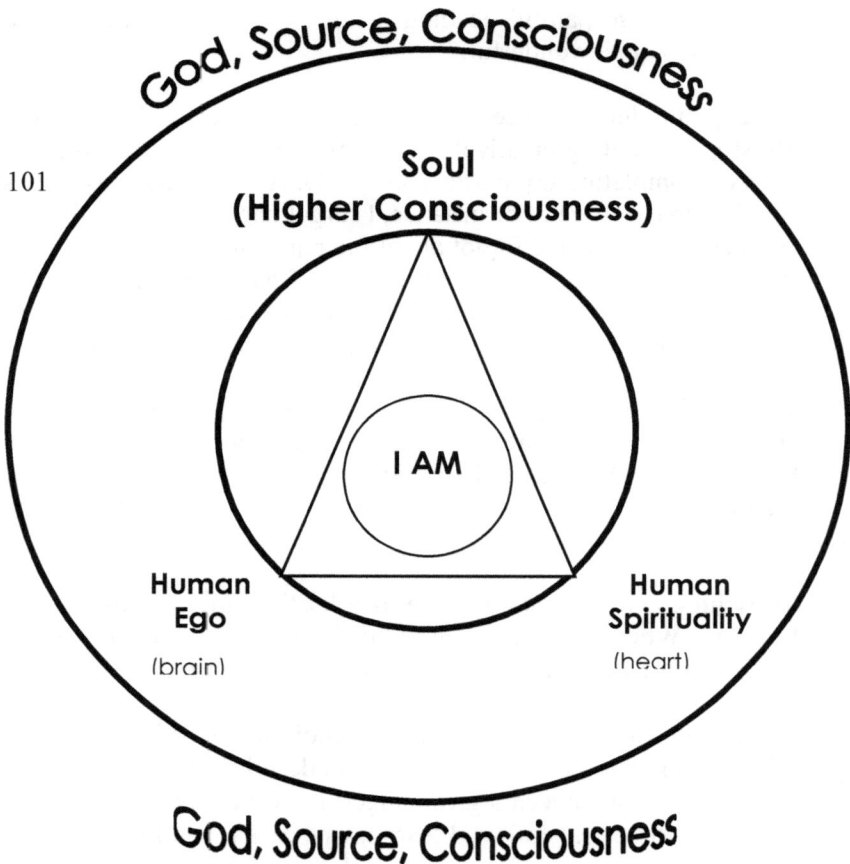

The model, they instructed, should illustrate the constant existence of **God/ Source/ Consciousness** as the creator of the universe and thus, the creator of all.

Our souls (or higher consciousness) are 'plugged in' to God and are in continuous, ongoing communion with God in the ether. Many religions refer to the ether as heaven. My guides promised that one day they would teach me more about heaven.

Our **soul (or higher consciousness)** seeks divine spirituality and is continuously learning from God and other spiritual beings. Our soul also seeks oneness with our human spirituality (earthly life) and learns from our human experience, each time we 'sign up' for a human life.

Thomas encouraged me to see learning as circular, regenerative, generative and reciprocal. As we live our human lives, we are engaged in an ongoing learning and teaching process. We both learn from and teach new things to our higher consciousness, and the same is true in reverse. This continuous learning (or enlightenment) allows us to connect with God and others at a deeper level for the purpose of giving and receiving love.

Integral to our human experience is our ego, and our human spirituality. They are a little like yin and yang in that the ego can take us to very dark places. Our human spirituality can act as an empath that keeps us caring and connected.

The **ego** is very important and when balanced with our human spirituality and in communion with our higher consciousness, helps us understand who we are. This gives us a sense of identity and confidence. It also provides a healthy sense of self-worth and self-awareness. Thomas reminded me that it is important for us to honor our ego.

He also reminded me that as human beings, balancing our ego is an ongoing challenge. More often, it is out of balance. This is when we struggle with over-confidence (or under-confidence), the illusion of an individual existence separate from creation and others, and the belief that we must fight for ourselves in the world. The ego is often associated with the mind and sense of time, neither of which allows us to know our true selves or live in, and appreciate the present.

An unbalanced ego results in fear. Fear is conflict. Fear causes us to desire control. Fear is typically the basis for egotistical behavior. In this space a continuous struggle between, "I know more than you" and "what if I don't know enough to control [my life] or [the situation] or [another person] exists. Also in this space, we are not open to feedback which is the foundation of learning. We frequently judge others and ourselves harshly, and are unable to listen, or hear others. These conditions allow for zero growth and create pain, either for ourselves, or others, or both.

Thomas helped me understand our **human spirituality** with three words: an open, aspiring heart. This is where love resides, he said. Love is experienced in many ways: compassion, empathy, forgiveness, gratitude, harmony, peace, balance, openness, generosity and friendship are all expressions and experiences of love. The result is a lightness of spirit, joy, knowledge, connectedness to others (in all forms) and greater wisdom. Our ego and human spirituality require balance in order to serve us; otherwise we are ruled by ego.

Thomas and others emphasized the word *symbiosis*. When balanced (or in a state of symbiosis) our ego and human spirituality work together to achieve the goals and desires of our soul. A blended ego and human spirituality allows us to be guided by our higher consciousness and to enter into a partnership of learning with and from one another. The result is greater wisdom, greater joy, and greater love. When this happens, we achieve our goal; we become who we were intended to be, thus, God is as much in us as external to us. We then become a part of the great **I AM**.

"I AM" is a powerful and empowering statement that allows us to embrace who we are fully, to find our voice, and to enter into our divine work or purpose without separation from God or others.

৯৯৯৯৯

The day came when I realized that nothing else I know how to do has ever felt like the thrill I experience when I sing sacred music. When I sing, the vibrations my singing creates brings my higher consciousness, human spirituality and ego into harmony with God. We achieve a symbiotic state and exist for those moments without separation.

This is a universal truth. Just replace 'singing' with whatever you love to do, and when you do it, there is no division between you and God. God doesn't care how well you do it, as long as you do it from your heart.

This is how I fell back in love with my poetry, my gift of writing, and myself. It no longer mattered whether I would ever be a great writer. It only matters that I write. And each time I sit down to write, I strengthen my skill, become a better writer, enjoy myself immensely and enter into a state of symbiosis with God. When we are in a state of symbiosis with God, we are at one with all.

When we do what we love, we achieve higher levels of vibration. Higher levels of vibration carry love farther, faster. The more we do what we love, the higher our vibration, the further our love travels and through this act we send out immeasurable amounts of healing into the world.

ৡৡৡ

Over the next three weeks, I edited some of my older poetry, cataloged my (aging) publications, and thoroughly enjoyed the way my poetry revealed who I had been. Even the bad poetry was evidence of growth. What remained was to write new poetry; poetry that would evidence who I am today.

A few days later, I wrote *One Love*. I rarely write in long hand, but the urge to hold a pen came over me so immediately, I pushed my computer aside. As I wrote, the ink skidded out of the pen and stroked the ambient images into words. To the best of my knowledge, this experience only took a few moments.

When it was over, I looked at what I'd written and couldn't believe it. Bitterly disappointed, I crumpled it into a ball and almost tossed it. *Absolute crap* I muttered, and quit the room.
The next day I looked at the crumpled ball several times wondering why I didn't just burn the damn thing until finally I picked it up and smoothed it open. There it was, so simple, really. I didn't know how I could have missed it. It only required one small edit to describe what all these months have taught me about love and light.

## One Love

> Before Consciousness
>     or air
> Before sea cliffs
>     or song
> Before anything was,
>     after every passing —
> From one ending
>     to the next beginning
> there is
>     only Love.
> One
>     Love.

**Late September, 2007**
In my next session I presented Trish with a spiral-bound copy of my poetry.
We hugged and exchanged tears of joy.

"So, *this* is what you've been up to," she exclaimed, jumping up and down
hugging the bound poems to her heart. "I was trying to tap in to you to
prepare for our session but your guides kept saying, 'we won't let you
connect with her right now'."

I was delighted to hear this. Delighted that my guides, who knew I wanted to
surprise Trish with this gift because I saw it as evidence of what an amazing
coach she is, would keep my secret. It was yet another lesson for me about
how our guides are wise, knowing, and 100% here for us. It was undeniable
proof of how much they love us. Even enjoy us.

"Time just disappeared," I said.

She nodded, "You bent time. They're showing me that you committed
yourself so fully to this project, time did not exist for you in typical human
dimension and that is why you were able to get done in three days what it
would typically take several weeks to complete. They'll teach you more
about bending time in the future."

"Who was helping me with this?" I asked. "My guides must have been
involved in every single moment, decision, action... I have never felt less
alone!"

"They're telling me that they actually stepped back."

"They did? But I *felt* them. I was *never* alone. I know I was guided every
step of the way!"

"Yes, you were being closely guided. But primarily by your ascended
masters. And Jesus. You see, this was a highly creative project and very
specific. Ascended masters work with us on very specific projects," she
reminded. "They asked your guides to respectfully step back so that they
could have full creative influence with you, and your guides agreed. They
never left you. They just stepped aside to allow others to guide your creative
energies."
The words *amaranthine love* came back to me as I listened to Trish. Just as
my guides had circled so many months earlier to surround me in their healing

energy while my soul and human spirituality reintegrated, I now understood that my ascended masters had been circling continuously to help me reintegrate with my poetry. Their circling created a vibration so beautiful that it inspired and sustained me throughout the project.

"And Jesus?" I whispered.

"Jesus was with you because this was a labor of love for you. It was bigger than falling back in love with your poetry. It was about falling back in love with yourself. Of being able to recognize yourself. To say, 'there I am, me, Rebecca' when you look in the mirror. They're telling me this was necessary in order for them to prepare you for the next step."

"Next step?" I've said it before, I am forever catching up in these sessions.

"Why writing, of course," she answered calmly. "Now that you've said 'yes' to your life's purpose, you've found your voice! "This," she said with an appreciative pat to my poetry, "this is just the start."

*";;;if we could see the miracle of a single flower clearly, our whole life would change.*

— Santiz

# *Wholeness*

**October, 2007**

I left Trish's that day wild with joy. She was right! I was alive with poetry and felt creatively gargantuan. But writing would have to wait. First, my sister and I were taking our Dad and his wife of 25 years to Texas to visit our brother, Ron. The last vacation we had ever taken as a family was when I was 13 years old, and Ron, who had already graduated from college and entered the Air Force, had not been with us.

I was doing about 70 miles an hour when suddenly I nearly swerved off the road because my mother came to me in one of the most intense impressions I've ever experienced. She wanted me to talk to my brother about my work with Trish. She asked me to repeat her words over and over until I got them right. Her message was simply, "tell your brother that I love him. Tell him how proud I am of him. Tell him that my fingerprints are all over him." I had to keep repeating this last part out loud because while the words were beautiful, it was not an easy expression to remember and I knew it was important to convey the message exactly as she intended.

So there I was driving the car at high speed with my mother (in spirit form) being bombarded with impressions so powerful that I almost couldn't see the road. I was trying to find words to match the impressions, say them out loud, and feel how my body responded in order to gauge whether I was getting the message right. And, I was crying. Her message (and her manner) was so tender yet fierce; her love all encompassing. I had always felt this much love from her and couldn't wait until my brother did, too.

Although I haven't talked about angels in this story, I know they exist and have felt their protection and guidance, often. Clearly they helped me keep the car on the road, and protected all who were in the vicinity that day!

စာ-စာ-စာ-စာ

I think I've already admitted that I'm not always brave. I have long enjoyed my brother's friendship and respect, and I wasn't sure how open he would be to this message from our mother. He has a fine mind and is intellectually trained to look at facts; to think scientifically. As excited as I was for him to feel the enormity of our mother's love, I was intimidated by what I anticipated would translate as a lack of facts. So I recruited my sister, Phyllis who had started sessions with Trish about six months earlier.

Phyllis understood our mother's message immediately and did not ask for facts. She didn't need to. She is the most intuitive of the three of us. Our mother's message, she said would 'heal two hearts lonesome for each other'.

When we approached my brother, we found him entirely receptive; in fact, he was rapt and listened without interruption. Afterward, we were all spent. We agreed to go to bed and sleep on it.

The next morning my brother sought me out. He said he'd called out to our mother before going to sleep, and acknowledged her message. He fell asleep almost immediately, and slept better than he'd slept in years. He awoke with a deeply peaceful feeling. He had no questions. It simply is what it is.

Love.

Immediately following my Texas vacation, I began to write.

# Chant

He speaks
In a voice six centuries past
and tells me
that in his lifetime
I was low born,
not allowed to speak beyond
a nod or bow.

I served in silence
and helped the braves prepare for hunt
by smoothing warm bear grease
over their bodies
to ease the drag of animal hide against
their warrior backs
and thighs.

When I was old enough
I noticed him —
the tall one
with the thick, black hair women
liked to touch,
and sanded voice
that left us drenched.

In silence, I watched
sun and shadow undulate
against the swell and hollow of his
long body
the way he swayed
when he talked to the wind
canted prayers for rain
and told us of things to come
with his wild drawings of two wolves,
circling

They said he was a soothsayer
living his last life
that he did not eat meat
had never known a woman
and spent his days cross-legged
in prairie grass, keeping vigil

In secret I visited his drawings
again and again
to trace their movements with my fingers
excited by the indomitable spirit of the wolves
until one day he came to me,
both antelope and bear —
graceful, hard

We circled like wolves
until I came alive inside
and began to chant
to feel the ecstasy of my voice
the swell of vibration
and know the thrill of making sound.

# Mariah Rising

I dreamed they came to me
with clasped hands
circling

Their touch ignited light streams
that arced across time
and domed the earth
in unbounded amnesty

"For you," they said,

Their heart-shaped faces
thrummed healing rhythms
that freed me from the nether

and 50 years of miasmic men —
a lifetime lived
rutting in the roots of trees
trying to drink air
suffocated
by dirt

I rose to the ether
like a Phoenix
where we moved effortlessly
through each other
performing pliés
to the faint smell
of cinnamon and myrrh

## Still

When the owl called long
after midnight
my cat went for cover
and I knew to listen for secrets —
        watch for you

She said you would crawl like night
into my dreams
melt 20 years in a moment with your
faded eyes and incarnadine fire
that hold no heat
or heart
        still

# Muse

He is an old man
not always able to remember who he was
before.

He knows his bones ache,
the room always feels cold,
and today, there's a dude with wings

hanging out in the corner
that no one else seems to see.
People visit and say things like,

"remember this one, Dad?"
and ask him what he'd like.
All he can think

is that he doesn't like anything
or anyone, except her —
and she never comes

Are they keeping her from him?

Sometimes he can get clear
and remember her bending over him
in the heartbeat of a moment,

before her breath brushes his face,
and he can almost see down the neck
of her dress —

feel the round, softness of her,
lightly kneading his chest.
Makes him rigid, and thankful to God,
all at once

They met during the war.
He was a peace worker,
she was in college.

One dance,
a near kiss that he couldn't forget in seven years.

He saw her again in 1949 when everyone,
determined to forget about the war
was making babies. Lost in her kisses,
and more kisses.

He wasn't her first
but she may as well have been his only.
He loved the way she was without abandon,
the way her breasts swelled in his mouth,
the way she hardly ever put on a robe
to answer the door.

The music came then, hard and fast
as if God had too many things to say
and couldn't pace Himself.
Night after night he tore himself from her
molten
and bent to his music until she came to him

with her soft begging.
They said his music was a "divine gift"
he was "chosen by God"
Things were so good,
but when he asked her to marry him
she slipped away.

Bereft, he thought the music would stop,
but instead had even more to say.
And so he wrote
endlessly
with no sense of time
for years, decades —
a lifetime,
accepting commissions and acclaim.

There were times
in any one of the crowds — the crowds all looked the same,
when he thought he saw her.

But it never was,
or maybe it was,
   he couldn't know for sure

   Until one day she was there, unchanged.

"You were always the one," he told her
She nodded gravely, agreeing
"It's the same with me,"

And even before he asked her
to never again leave him
he knew that she would

His music became
Eclectic
disorderly, unpredictable
and still they loved him.

It went on that way —
recognition, success, position
she would appear, just as before.

He can't remember for how long,
or how many times,
or where she is today,
or what today is —
But in those moments when he can get clear
he remembers that all his music,
every note,
even those written before he met her,
wasn't for her, or about her,
or even because of her —

His music was her.

# Summer Sprites

Night falls,
summer night
when the last red streaks leave the sky
Gaia opens to ether
what she cannot hold

You and I, summer sprites
stroke the sea, skim the sky,
like twin tides in twirl
unbounded,
these sweet summer nights

And at autumn's eve
you take my hand
mortal again
Every season ends.

# Like the Shoulder of a Child

There comes a moment
like the soft slope
of a hill
when
summer is grown
her warm smiles and fertile mornings
evaporate
          into fall  —
like the shoulder of a child
disappearing 'round a corner

and, in the winter
she'll be a woman.

# The Child Within

There is a child waking
within.
A sleepy-eyed child with tumbled curls
and that sleep-soft look
still on her face.
She takes me by the hand
leading me into the light,
almost dancing as she does,
Laughing
at the simplest things.

And she tells me
with her cherub's smile
that I really
must
get to know her

# Lovespeak

Energy
designed to wound
or warm
to wind around hidden curves
and wander into private moments
To palliate or promise

They are mistrals that shift the heart
and leave us windswept —
waiting

Let me step into
the wilds of your words
wear them like lingerie
exquisite, reckless

# Fuelling

A capricious summer wind
squeezes zigs of rain
through the pumping screen
where two bodies, frescoed and
folded into the softest
of hiplocks
ride the long glide,
and burble monosyllabic
moans

— the coffee waits

# Blowin' Smoke

Them old flames
lickin' at me again
like some kind of spirit

I keep waitin'
Figure they just gonna burn
'til they can't no more
burnin' on plenty
of fresh tinder
'cause my heart is so smoky, maybe
from the slow sounds
I keep thinkin' we'd make

Like the crazy wail
of a saxophone
just because the man
curls his lips
an' blows
Smokin'
an' hot

The kind iced lemonade won't cool
deep in the dog days of August

an' you
All sultry
an' ready

an' me
... burnin'

# After Eight

She's been gone a long time, now
Yet I remember that airless, glassy
summer when I was 12 —

Every time I turned a corner
they'd be whispering
wearing mean looks,
        the old hens
'til finally when winter came,
 she up and left
 sayin' it was just too damn cold!

I saw her once
standing at the edge of a jagged sea drop
letting the wind tangle her hair
and catch at the slender length of green
she wore around her neck
until unwound,
the freed thing lifted and floated over the edge
She was laughing that day
so much, her shoulders trembled
until the strap of her dress
slid off the slope of her shoulder
        naked

After awhile
most everyone forgot.
I guess a good story can sure grow stale quick.
But even though I was only a boy of 12
I knew what had them all a-buzz.

She had this smile,
teasing-like
the kind you put on for a man
after eight in the evening
        when moments are opaque
        and morning
            is a lifetime away.

# How Many Lives

Sometimes —
when she looks at him
she wonders how many lives
they'll spend together
it hangs in the air, ripe —
like an accidental touch
    knowing what she can't remember

Sometimes —
she remembers what she can't know
like the feel of coarse muslin
and the weight
of a hand-stitched quilt
the cool heat of a winter fire
    and his clean smile

they were prairie farmers
or migrant workers
she knows, because when his hands fold
soft around hers
    she can feel their labor

Sometimes —
she wonders
if they'll go on this way
stepping through time, together
    until they get it right

# Blue

One morning
I awoke to a behemothic
blue bed
My husband went to work
without a word
    never even glanced my way

The maid came and
made the bed with me in it —
just went about her business
despite my
    silent
        protests,
            the chippie

as if I she couldn't see me
among the 800 thread count
and square folds —
smaller than a speck
    speckless

When she came to strip the bed
on laundry day
I was balled up,
tossed down the chute
and promptly buried under
my husband's boxers
    and other soiled discards

I should have been worried about
time in the washer
but in order to worry
there must be expectation
    So easy to be
        a speck

The spin cycle gave me a little trouble
Still, I felt almost cogent
when I emerged
so I tried to think of the dryer
    as a vacation somewhere
        in the southwest

But I was
just a speck
that might blow away like top soil
    at any moment
        and become lost
            with the other specks

# From the Eaves

Some winters
like men,
are harder than others.
You can tell
by the Bastille-like
stalactites —

Daggers that hang heavy
from the eaves
like frozen bruises
that won't go away
until the spring melt,

And even then
may leave a few scars

## Leave-Taking

Each night for four nights before
Daniel Thomas missed the curve
he dreamed --
the dreams followed him long into day.

In the first dream, he saw
Archangel Michael
guide the safe landing of every airplane
coming into Detroit.
Daniel Thomas had never been to Detroit,
rarely traveled,
didn't usually remember dreams,
and was vaguely irritated when the
dream came back to him
over his morning coffee,
his drive to work,

his mid-morning meeting with Finance,
lunch with a sales rep from Moline,
and was still with him
on his drive home that evening.

On the second night, he dreamed of
Elijah scaling the clouds in his
incarnadine chariot.
Daniel Thomas hadn't read the
Old Testament in years,
didn't usually remember dreams,
and got to thinking of one or two
other stories he'd learned as a child.

On the third night, he watched as he
kissed his wife a tearful goodbye, and
contemplated the empty suitcase
spread open across the bed.
No matter how hard he tried, he
couldn't think what to pack.

In the morning, he wondered where
his wife had stored their suitcases,
and considered the possibility of a vacation.

On the fourth night he dreamed of
his older brother Brian, who was lost
in the tangles of Viet Nam in 1972,
and never found.
No words passed between them as
they tossed back beers for the first time,
bathed in his brother's refulgent smile.

On the fifth day when Daniel Thomas
missed the curve
he floated like Elijah in a chariot
guided by Archangel Michael,
saw his sleeping wife, who was not yet
aware of his sudden departure,
and understood why the suitcase
had been empty.

He would need nothing, now --
Nothing but to take Brian's outstretched hand
so as not to miss this next curve.

## Winter Leaf

I kicked at a winter leaf
as it blew underfoot
It sighed
and skittered on
Like an old soul
free

*"The glory of friendship is not the outstretched hand, nor the kindly smile,*
*nor the joy of companionship; it's the spiritual inspiration that comes to*
*one when [she] discovers that someone else believes in [her]."*
— Ralph Waldo Emerson

# *Harmony*

In November 2007, someone I greatly admired, did not know well, yet had always felt close to, passed away. He was a highly accomplished, dignified, giant of a man who had enjoyed a good life, a successful career as a composer, musician and teacher, but sadly had suffered from Alzheimer's for nearly a decade before his passing. I could never explain the closeness we felt for each other, except that we both loved sacred choral music and poetry. When I learned of his passing, I contacted Trish to ask if it had been peaceful.

"Very peaceful," she said. "Entirely peaceful. He was ready to leave. Oh, in fact," she added, "he visited you as he was leaving this world."

"He did?" I was astonished!

"Yes," she confirmed. "He wanted to say 'good-bye'."

I was both moved and honored. I had always thought of our connection as something that was very nice to have. Now, I began to understand that it had been something of great value. Had I missed a lesson or an opportunity of some sort?

Over the next month I began to experience many indistinct impressions of him and found myself wondering more and more about why we had enjoyed such a heartfelt connection. Because of his Alzheimer's, we hadn't spoken in at least seven years; possibly more. So why was I feeling aware of him now, unless there was more he wanted to say? Finally, I asked Trish about it.

Trish looked to my guides and her eyes popped with surprise. "Oh! Your mother has just come forward. She says he has a very specific message for you. His message is, 'bring your gifts into the world—share your gifts'."

My hand fluttered to my heart as a surprised "Oh!" escaped.

"There's more here but it's really complex," Trish continued, talking rapidly. "I can't understand everything he's telling me. Wait, your mother is helping. It's a treble clef—oh I get it. He's drawing a treble clef in the air and your mother is saying he wants to keep working with you. Your paths crossed so late in his life that he was cognitively incapable of completing your work together. Now that he's passed, he's using his musical ability to help women in the ether open their fifth chakra and express themselves more freely—Oh! Okay, he's helping them 'find their voice'. Get it Rebecca? 'Find their voice'."

And there it was; the message my guides had been giving me lately. My journey over the past year had been all about learning who I am and understanding my life's purpose; or to express it another way, 'to find my voice'. This realization lay wide open and bare to me.

"Yes, okay," Trish continued, confirming what I was already beginning to understand. "Now your mother is saying his work was to help you find your creative voice and bring it to the world. He has some music he has composed for you and wants to bring through. It will help the two of you continue your work together. The music will provide inspiration and healing."

"It will also open your chakras," she continued, "and will be good for mental acuity. He lost his in this lifetime in order to learn how to teach others how to regain and sharpen theirs. He is a master in this regard. He keeps repeating 'sooner rather than later. Share your gifts with the world sooner rather than later'. He wants you to know that just as he is a gifted musician, you are a gifted poet. The way he brings through his music is the same process you use to bring through your poetry."

Of course by now I was a mass of cascading tears. To experience such love and devotion flow from another dimension is beyond description. To know that there is so much support, guidance and direction from those who are in spirit, reinforced for me that love never dies; it simply changes energy.

In some ways it had become easy to believe that my mother loves me from 'beyond the grave' because she's family. But now I was learning that this great man who had been so respected in his field, and so influential as a mentor in the lives of many young musicians, is a soul whom I have known throughout the ages. We are connected through a bond of ageless friendship; endless union.

There was just one problem. Neither Trish nor I know how to channel music. Yet just as we were both wondering how to accomplish this, my guides reminded Trish that she has a colleague, Tony, who has this ability. Within ten days' time, the music had been successfully channeled, downloaded, and recorded to a CD.

I met Tony the day I went to pick up the music. My first impression was entirely about his eyes which are intensely blue. Within that intensity lies his gift of music. Channeling music is an exhaustive process that involves using the physical body as an instrument for the music. Tony was physically spent yet spiritually exhilarated.

"Thank you for this opportunity," he said, offering a hug. "Your friend is amazing—a master. I feel as though I learned so much from him—new techniques for translating and integrating music with healing."

Unsure about what to expect, the first time I listened to the music there was just the smallest sense of disappointment. The music comprised simple and seemingly uncomplicated tones. I wondered what all the fuss was about. Yet the past twelve months had been about opening myself to new truths of the universe; about making intentional change through experiencing my spirituality. I had spent my life being entirely controlled by my ego, first through emotion and later through intellect. My current journey was to embrace my spiritually and connect with life.

As I opened to this new experience, I learned that toning is a way of increasing our physical energy by removing toxins and healing the body. The use of a combination of tones and rhythmic sounds can alter our vibrations to accelerate healing and increase harmony. As I learned this, I was reminded that in 1999 when I underwent major surgery, my Western-educated surgeon recommended I bring a portable CD player and my favorite CD.

"Research studies show that patients heal up to three times faster if we expose them to the music of their choice during and immediately after surgery," she explained. "Bring something uplifting," she added.

Through the toning process we connect on a deeper level with God (if we use the model for spiritual connectedness and fulfillment provided earlier, this is one way we enter into the 'I AM' state) and experience transformation emotionally, physically and spiritually. Toning allows energy to move freely through us, increases our feeling of well-being and thus, expands our openness. Our ability to be open is in direct proportion to our ability to reach our human potential (find our voice, fulfill our life's purpose) and increases both internal and external harmony.

The above explains why singing is such an enjoyable, transformative experience for me.

This new knowledge, and the love in my heart for the soul who cared enough to connect with me after his passing, helped me to understand that my human expectations or assumptions for what this music would be like, were baseless. I began to listen to the music which is a series of seven movements, every day.

Seven is a sacred number for me. After listening to the music for seven days I was led to write this book, and to call it *Ariana Sings: One Woman's Journey to Find Her Voice*.

*"You don't **have** a soul. You **are** a soul. You **have** a body."*
— C.S. Lewis

# *The Divineness of Being Human*

## Cellular Memory

Cellular memory is a concept over which there is currently a lot of controversy. Traditional western medicine typically does not recognize cellular memory. My guides have shared that in fact memories, habits, tastes, and interests can be stored in our cells, much like we store them in our brain. Cellular memory is one of the ways we are able to learn more each time we come into body, while we retain previous learning.

My sister, Phyllis learned from her guides recently that after she 'signed up' to do another life, she was so excited about coming back into body, she forgot that we all come into this world as vulnerable babies. Before we can begin working on our life's purpose, we have to begin the process of remembering. For some, this happens very naturally. For others, it takes a lifetime. My guides tell me that, "it takes as long as it takes." Her soul, upon being born into a human baby said, "Rats! I forgot about this part. Now I have to learn all these basic things all over again before I can get down to business."

Today, she is one of the most gifted, intuitives I know. Her work is to create soul quilts, memory quilts, legacy quilts and story quilts for people to help them connect with the stories of their lives, and thus understand better their soul's desire. What is amazing is that she does this entirely by listening to her guides, and the guides of her clients. No one taught her to knit, to crochet, to sew or design patterns. Everything she does is original.

Now, how did she learn to do this entirely on her own? One answer is cellular memory. In many previous lifetimes, she was a tailor, seamstress, weaver, or designer. She has the soul of an artist and in this lifetime, she is a

121

fiber artist. She carries the memories of many lifetimes as an artist in her cells as well as her intuition, and this has not only helped her to remember who she is, but because she remembers, she can move her artistry forward.

My guides also said that before we come into this world, we make agreements with all who have signed up to support us so that we can 'recognize' them when our paths cross here on earth. Sometimes we do this more successfully than other times. Can you remember a time you felt as though you knew someone, but in fact, you'd never met them before ... in *this* lifetime?

In his book, *The Heart's Code*, Paul Pearsall (1998) provides scientific evidence that the heart thinks, remembers and speaks to the brain about feelings, and connects to other hearts. Thinking from the heart helps us balance our intellect with our intuition and allows those cellular messages to come through.

It's often easy to think of our human lives as difficult. I've heard it said often enough that this life isn't for the faint of heart. In my most depressed moments I have even believed this to be true. Not long ago, I received disappointing news several days in a row. As a result I felt myself sinking into a depressed state. I thought, "Not again!" For two days I struggled to fight the depression. It was the first time in more than a year. I was frightened and began to doubt myself. Then, on the third day, my depression lifted.

"*Really*? What *was* that?" I asked my guides. I could feel them smile. I could even feel them stroking my head.

"Little one," they said (and again, their counsel comes to me in impressions, not words), "Your human personality swings because you have so much passion. You will always have brief periods of depression here and there but you will never be stuck there again. You said 'yes' to your life's purpose. Saying 'yes'—remembering who you are and why you came into this world, and agreeing to fulfill that purpose, has set you free."

I believe there is much, much more to our human lives than we may realize.

As spiritual beings engaged in a human experience, there's a reason we choose to return to human form, over and over again. While I believe it's true that we come back to learn lessons, to overcome fears, and to resolve things we did not resolve in former lifetimes, we also come back to help others, to expand our knowledge, to help our soul grow more wise through our human interactions; to spread love.

As importantly, I believe there is something about being human that is wonderful beyond words, and exclusive to being in body. We do amazing things in spirit form. We know so much *more* in spirit form. Yet there is something about being in body that causes our light to grow even brighter. When our spirit is placed in our human body, we encounter a different kind of sanctity; the sanctity of form—it is the ultimate act of empowerment because we *chose* to come back into body—to learn more and to love more. In human form, our light grows even brighter in order to help, connect with, and bring other humans, and at times even out-of-body souls, into a joyful experience.

**Divine Light**
One day in August, 2007 my friend's dog, Capri was acting up so badly I suggested she make an appointment with a well-known animal communicator, Lena Swanson. During the session Lena indicated that an earthbound spirit inhabited my friend's kitchen, and this was disturbing to Capri.

"The earthbound spirit is not harmful but she does treat Capri with disrespect. She is all about hierarchy and believes that a human spirit out of body is higher in the hierarchy of life, than a dog spirit in body. So, Capri and the earthbound spirit are in constant conflict. You might consider doing a little ritual and inviting the earthbound spirit into the light. At the very least, you can tell her respectfully that she isn't welcome in your home and needs to leave."

A few days later, my friend and I decided to do exactly that. Just as we were wrapping up the ritual and inviting the earthbound spirit into the light, the wind lifted and blew straight through the house. I looked at my friend. My friend looked at me. Neither one of us had a clear sense about whether we'd been successful, but we took the wind as a positive sign.

in a session with Trish a few days later, I started to tell her about this experience. Trish nodded, but I could tell she was distracted. Finally I stopped relating the details and asked, "What is going on?"

Trish smiled and said, "The earthbound spirit's name is Lula and she is with you right now. Here's what happened. When you spoke to her about the light, your own light grew so bright, she was attracted to it. You spoke with such respect, gentleness and kindness that she was attracted to your light rather than the larger light, and she wanted to be with you. So she followed you home."

"The next day," she continued, "Lula followed you to work, but once there she was repelled by the high levels of activity and business drive that exist in your workplace. She's showing me that she literally put her hands to her ears and screamed as she left. But she keeps returning to you when you're not at work."

"As you've been telling me about the ritual you performed, I've been telling Lula in no uncertain terms that she may not attach to you, and I've been showing her the light. She is starting to see past your light now. Your light and your kindness reminded her that what she wants does exist; she just didn't know how to get there. There she goes. She is with the light now."

"So, what was the wind all about, then?" I asked.

Trish smiled. "You asked for confirmation that you were doing the right thing. You manifested the wind as confirmation."

"But I wasn't doing the right thing... we didn't get the job done."

"You *were* doing the right thing," Trish affirmed. "You were caring for a lost soul. You just needed a little more information about how to do it effectively."

Now, the idea of earthbound spirits hanging around is a little creepy to me, but this next story helped me to put it into a context I can appreciate.

ༀ-ༀ-ༀ-ༀ

One day Trish said to my sister, "They're telling me you need to go buy a book and they're recommending you go to Orr Books, are you familiar with it?" Orr Books was a quiet, privately-owned bookstore located for nearly forty years in the legendary uptown area of urban Minneapolis; an area best known for its lakes and late nineteenth-century architecture.

So, Phyllis went to the uptown area but was unable to locate the bookstore. She wandered around asking directions until someone told her that the bookstore had recently closed its doors and no longer existed. She was both disappointed that she wouldn't be picking up the book that day, and surprised that Trish had made an error. We'd never known Trish to make an error.

In her next session Phyllis told Trish why she hadn't been able to get the book. Trish looked confused for a brief moment and then said, "Oh! Here's what they're showing me. There was an earthbound spirit who had been wandering in the uptown area for centuries. Your guides sent you to that area because they knew this earthbound spirit would resonate with the vibrations from your light. As you walked around the area looking for the bookstore, this earthbound spirit watched you and in those moments grew warm and open because your light was so lovely. Finally, he was able to see the larger light and was drawn to it because the loveliness of your light led him there. He crossed over that day because of your light."

When I told this story to one of my friends, she commented that it sounded like Trish just got it wrong, and then tried to cover it up with the story about being the light for an earthbound spirit. And why shouldn't she think that? She doesn't know Trish, and we are programmed to be suspicious. I didn't know exactly how to respond to her, but her comment kept coming back to me for several days.

Finally I asked, "why does this keep coming back to me?"

The answer I received over the course of several days is that whether or not we're listening to our guides, we often get some of it right—and some of it wrong. In this case, the book was recommended to Phyllis by her guides, and her light was needed to help an earthbound spirit. Two different things—both important. But the messages came so close together, it was interpreted as one message. We often combine more than one message and then spend whatever time is needed to unwind them until we get it right. And, during the unwinding, we learn so much.

Again, the idea of earthbound spirits following us around can seem a little creepy because it's foreign to us. But the idea that we can help spirits who are out of body, *as well as* human beings, adds dimension to our existence, and breadth to our purpose. We are here for all. Love, light and life are not commodities unique to the human experience!

**Divinely Human**

There is something about being in body that is divine, simply because we are human. Meredith Hall, author of *Without a Map* (2007) wrote,

> "This body I know loves to lie stretched on its side, reading. This body I live inside loves to burst into a sprint to retrieve my wallet from the car. To tease the dog with a romp. To dance when no one is home, the childhood ballet poses—arabesques, pirouettes, fifth position. To make love in the light of winter sun, goose-fleshed and generous."

To this I would add that it is only in body that we can revel in the taste of a spicy bolognaise accompanied by a smooth red wine with a jaunty finish. These are the *just desserts* of being human.

Not long ago a medical doctor told me that my family history of hypertension had caught up with me. She wrote out a prescription which I dutifully had filled. I didn't like the way the prescription bottle felt in my hand. I didn't like the way my throat seemed to close up against the idea of swallowing the pill. I absolutely hated how the drug made me feel. I experienced nearly every kind of side effect you can imagine and wanted to stop taking the drug. The doctor assured me that this drug could not possibly cause those side effects and in fact, increased the drug from five milligrams to 10 milligrams to 20 milligrams.

Every night my stomach retched when it was time to take the drug. In addition to hating the medication, I was angry with my body; angry that it needed a drug. Angry that it was not adjusting to the drug it needed. I felt as if my body was failing me.

After two-and-a-half weeks of illness from the drug, I was rushed to the emergency room. My lips had swollen to five times their normal size and my throat was slowly closing. My body was allergic to the drug and could no longer tolerate it. It took three days for me to stabilize.

During those three days, the same message kept coming to me; first from the emergency room doctors, then from the various medical staff who helped me to recover. Each in a different way, said, 'isn't the body a marvelous thing?! It tries to tell us when something isn't right and when we don't get the message, it just keeps doing things until we finally listen'.

This was one of the most insightful paradigm shifts I can ever remember encountering. My body wasn't failing me, it was saving me! Once I began to realize that my body was serving me rather than failing me, I could embrace what was happening and participate in making healthier choices. As divine human beings, our bodies have the ability to tell us what we need, and what isn't working for us. I kept following the doctor's instructions about the medication because I listened from my intellect, only. My intellect said, 'she is a medical doctor and it's her job to know what my body needs'. Yet my heart, through intuition had been telling me for nearly three weeks that the medication wasn't right for my body. I had not been listening to my heart. It nearly cost me my life.

I am grateful to the medical profession for all the care and expertise they have given me in my life. And, because we are spiritual beings engaged in a divine human experience, the message here is that we need to listen to both our intellect *and* our intuitive hearts in order to truly understand what is best for us.

This is one example of what I mean when I say that it is indescribably divine to be human.

# *One Love*

How to end a story that has no end? There is so much more to tell. The light of remembering is gradual; I learn a little more every day. But they're telling me it's time to wrap it up so that it can be shared with the world sooner rather than later. This is not an ending; merely a pause.

What I find amazing every time I think about it is that everything Nancy said has all come true. She foretold of a change coming in my career. She said I was done with my organization unless I found a way to rekindle my passion. If she had not called this out, I think it's unlikely I would have been able to speak my truth when Linda asked me if I wanted the sales manager position. If I hadn't spoken my truth, where would I be today?

I couldn't know that I would learn how essential passion is to my human existence. Without passion, I become confused about who I am. When I am confused, I can't pursue what I love, and I no longer send out loving and healing vibrations into the world. When we send nothing out, we get little or nothing back. We may still be breathing, but on some level, we have ceased to exist. We are still loved, supported and guided, but we are not empowered. To live joyfully as a spiritual being engaged in a human experience requires that we embrace empowerment.

Also amazing is that even though Nancy told me this would happen, it wasn't a foregone conclusion. At every point I had choices, and those choices led to other choices, discoveries, opportunities and truths. But the enjoyment that lay in the fulfillment of these choices, discoveries, opportunities and truths came to me by embracing empowerment.

Nancy said I would write about something very different than I ever thought I would write about. So true! I couldn't know that the most important learning I've ever done is happening right now. The world is changing. More and more people are listening to their hearts and asking questions we never dared to ask before. Perhaps it's because so many of us are older souls now.

I mentioned in the introduction to this book that my intent isn't to try to convince you—it is only to share. You decide for yourself what to believe. The greatest truth I have learned is this: we are spiritual beings engaged in a human experience. We exist because of love—to give love and to be loved—before anything was—after every passing—from one ending to the next beginning. Because there is only love.

One love.

In body, we have an opportunity to be the bowl; open and receptive to understanding the messages from our guides and other spiritual beings. As the bowl, we learn to listen in a new way—with soft ears, the way we are learning to look at the world with soft eyes. By listening in this manner, what we hear first is that everything is love. We live because of love—the universe exists because of love. Each of us has a unique role. Each of us is integral to the effectiveness of this loving network. Every soul has a purpose without which the universe is incomplete.

What we hear next is the question, 'what kind of bowl are you'? Be the bowl!

## *Joyful remembering!*

July, 2008

*"Rules for happiness: someone to love, something to do, and something to hope for."*

—18th century philosopher, Immanuel Kant

# *Epilogue*
# *Love is Unstoppable*

One morning about two years after I released **Ariana Sings**, my guides suggested I write an epilogue and re-release the book. When I asked them why, they said, "Because finding your voice is one thing—learning to use it is the next part of your journey."

છે છે છે છે

All my life, I've been a romantic. For example, the first time I saw the snow-covered Rockies I was nearly knocked out by what a romantic backdrop they made. I may have been slightly influenced by the fact that I was thoroughly in love at the time.

The first time I saw the White House I was struck by the romanticism of the many lives—leaders—drama—and life-changing decisions that structure has given shelter to.

When I was six or seven, I tried on my first pair of roller skates—the kind that clipped to the bottom of my shoes—and was instantly enamored with them because I realized how fast those skates would take me down the street to see Kenny, the love of my life.

Romance is everywhere and in nearly everything.

As a teenager, I loved to read and devoured the classics, contemporary fiction, sci-fi, and of course, romance novels. In my young adult years

Kathleen E. Woodiwiss released *The Flame and the Flower* and brought the romance genre out of hiding and into the blazing sunlight for all to read. The genre exploded, delivering to readers palpitations of every imaginable kind. Yet those books didn't just offer vicarious sex—they delivered handsome heroes, courtly romance, buckets of unrequited love, and the promise of an end so satisfying that for just a moment the world was brighter—often through the glitter of tears.

One day in the spring of 1989, I decided I would write a romance novel. And so I did. I called it *When the Time is Right*. I sent it off to a number of publishers and received a fistful of rejections. I made changes and tried again. More rejections. Recently I ran across a musty-smelling copy of it and I laughed all the way through it because it was so awful. Really, the only thing to do was enjoy how sweetly terrible it was, and be grateful that no publisher had ever thought 'the time was right'.

But I hadn't gotten it out of my system yet and so the next year I wrote a second novel, *Maestro's Melody*. This one had a potentially good plot, but was written only slightly better than the first. I tried to get that story right for about five years, but the end result was still rejection. So, not only was the time not right, but the melody was flat as well.

At that point, I stopped trying to write a romance novel—even though I still loved them—even though I ached to be a romance author. Soon after that, I launched my game plan for earning a college degree. My undergraduate at a college for working adults was such a rewarding and compelling experience, it whetted my appetite for more. For the next nearly twenty years, I spent my time pursuing more education and a career—entirely focused on things that I believed were very serious and substantive. My heart still ached to be a romance author, but I no longer recognized this desire.

### Ariana, my joyful and irrepressible soul
My sister-in-law, Wanda is a spiritual massage therapist and healer. She and my brother were visiting me about four months after I first released *Ariana Sings*. They happened to come during a time I was wrestling a bit with my old nemesis, the Big D. She offered to give me an adjustment—a form of massage that connects with the soul.

I'm not one who raves about massage, but this experience was phenomenal. As she worked over me, I felt myself completely let go. I had no sense of time. I barely even felt her hands. Once in awhile I would hear her giggle softly under her breath. When we were done, she stepped back, and I saw wonder in her eyes.

She said, "Rebecca, you have a joyful soul."

I wanted to believe her, but I was convinced it wasn't true. The Big D visited so frequently, I was certain that no matter how "enlightened" I may have become through all of my spiritual work, my soul was dark. I would never be truly happy because my soul was so heavy.

But as I looked into her eyes, I saw that she was still communing with her celestials, and I realized they were speaking to me *through* her. Suddenly, I felt how she felt to have experienced the joy of my soul. In that moment, I knew it was true. My soul was beyond joyful—it was irrepressible.

After their visit, I was naive enough to think I was going to be happy from that point forward. Yet, everywhere I looked, things were in a state that didn't make me happy. I sustained a foot injury that kept getting worse instead of better, until I was temporarily disabled and had to stay off my feet entirely. The economy tanked. I had a job change about which I felt resentful, convinced I wasn't qualified to do the new job.

Throughout my complaints my guides kept saying, "Feeling joy is a choice."

"Really? I'm not sure I buy it. It's a lot of work to choose over and over again to be happy. Sometimes it doesn't feel possible."

Each time they would remind me, "You can re-up to be happy every day, or wallow in dissatisfaction. Which is harder?"

After several months of pain and disability, I brought it up in a session with Trish. She smiled patiently and said, "The left side of the body represents the past. Your foot is telling you that you have unresolved issues. It won't let you have freedom of movement until you resolve those issues."

I looked at her wondering where to begin and shook my head thinking, *how unfortunate to be so entirely knocked off my path by an injury, the economy and an ill-fitting job.*

But had I really been knocked off my path? What if these events weren't obstacles at all? What if they actually helped to position me for the next phase of my life, but I just couldn't see it?

One day in April of 2009 I was so frustrated, bored and fed up with the pain, I shrieked to no one in particular, "What do you *want* from me?"

My guides came in strongly and said, "It isn't what we want from you. It's what you want *for* yourself."

Moments later *Maestro's Melody* popped into my head. I groaned. I think I even said out loud, "You've *got* to be kidding. Are you really suggesting that I dig that thing out and try it again?"

### I was a closet writer
With a long-suffering sigh, I went to my laptop embarrassed to admit even to myself that I was trying (yet again) to write a romance novel. I was the very definition of a closet writer! My fingers burned as they skimmed across the keyboard of my computer deep into the night. I rose long before dawn each morning rewriting *Maestro's Melody*. I'd like to tell you that my foot stopped hurting, but in fact, it got worse. Still, I was having an amazing experience with the story—it kept unfolding, one surprise after another, making me laugh and sigh and fall in love with my characters all over again.

Then one day, I was done. I had loved writing it so much, it was sweet agony to be done. Yet there was such satisfaction to have finally told the story that had lived in my heart for twenty years.

My guides began to whisper two words softly into my ear, "The Loft."

My hands turned clammy. I knew what they meant. The Loft is a literary center in Minneapolis for writers. It has an excellent reputation. They were encouraging me to take a class and learn more about writing in the romance genre. I figured this probably meant I wasn't done writing *Maestro's Melody* after all. But my foot hurt, I wasn't very mobile, and it meant actually putting my dream on the line and finding out if I was any good at writing romances. If I took a class, it would either force me out of the closet, or remain there forever.

So, I shook my head. "No way."

"The Loft." It came to me over and over.

"Nope. No way!"

I had just started seeing Marcie New, a doctor of chiropractic and spiritual healer, who was using micro current on my feet. For the first time in eight months, I had begun to experience some relief. One day during a session she said to me, "Have you ever taken a course at The Loft? You might want to check that out."

I almost fell off the table.

Really, they are relentless sometimes, aren't they, those guides of ours?

So, I looked up The Loft's course offerings on the Internet. Sure enough, an evening class was starting the following week that focused on writing women's fiction and in particular, the romance novel. The course required students to have a completed manuscript for critique. It was a perfect fit.

I went to the class with a very specific purpose in mind—to learn where and how to submit my manuscript to publishers. About two-and-a-half minutes into the class the instructors said, "This class isn't about learning where and how to submit your novel."

I thought, *Rats. This was a mistake. I wonder if I have the nerve to get up and walk out of here. I can still get a portion of the tuition back.*

"This class is about helping you focus and tighten your writing so that the right things pop in the right places. To begin, we'd like each of you to tell us about your book in no more than three or four sentences. The point is to hook us so that we want to know more about your book. Jot a few key phrases down and let's get started."

Stay or go? My brain was a blank. How could I describe my story in three-to-four sentences? I glanced around. There were only six students in the class. If I left now, it would be so obvious. I didn't want to hurt anyone's feelings and I just didn't feel comfortable getting up to leave. So, I threw myself into the exercise. Surely I could do this, right? After all, my story had lived in my heart for twenty years!

I jotted several phrases down. With each phrase I grew less confident. None of them seemed very compelling. When it was my turn to talk, I was painfully inarticulate. I couldn't believe the sound of my own voice which had a little whine to it—as if I was begging them to love my story. I watched all seven of them—five students and two instructors drop their eyes and stop listening. I couldn't hold their attention about my story for a mere four to five sentences!

Suddenly, my ego, heart, brain and my guides flooded my head with messages all at once.

**My ego** was all bent out of shape. It said, "What the heck is going on here? I'm an experienced presenter. People love to listen to me. I've got a great, original story. How impolite of them not to listen!"

**My guides** were saying, "Dear One, it's not enough to write a story you love—you need to learn how to present it, how to market it… and oh-by-the-way, you're going to have to rewrite it again… because neither you or your manuscript are ready, yet."

**My heart** was saying, "Oh goody! I get to go back into that world and live in it some more! Yay me!"

**My brain** was saying, "Crap. This is harder than I thought!"

When the chatter inside me quieted, I realized I was exactly where I needed to be… but for reasons different than I had thought. I could either open up to this, or miss out on a great opportunity that might not come around again.

That class changed my life. I learned a new way to write and adopted a new approach to fiction. I used it to rewrite *Maestro's Melody*. When I was done, my best friend who often voices messages from my guides shook her head and said, "Great story—terrible title. It's just not right. I think the title will get in your way."

Whooie but I was in love with the title and I didn't want to let it go. But after about a week or so, it kept coming back to me that she was right. I renamed the novel *Naked Hope*. Then, although I was still embarrassed about writing romance novels, I put together a group of test readers. While they were test-reading, I asked my guides, "Why am I so embarrassed about this?"

What came to me was that for the past nearly twenty years, my intent had been to be very serious. To pursue and accomplish serious things. To be taken very seriously. It's why I immersed myself in education. I viewed writing romances as whimsical—certainly not a very serious undertaking. It didn't put forth a new philosophy. It didn't support a current theory. It didn't even put a new slant on a current theory. I caught myself asking, *who takes romance authors seriously?*

Finally I began to understand that if something wasn't serious (by my definition), I couldn't see the value in it because it didn't align with who I thought myself to be. Being serious led to accomplishment. Accomplishment was how I judged myself worthy. If I didn't accomplish enough, then I wasn't worthy. This in turn, only made me more embarrassed about loving to write romances.

I asked myself, why did I think accomplishments = worthiness, and why was my overarching goal in life to be taken seriously, when I'd learned that my soul was so joyously irrepressible? I had no answer—no idea how to resolve my love of writing romance novels with my need to be serious and accomplished.

One day, one of the test readers sent me an email with her feedback. In it she wrote,

> "I must say that you have a wonderful gift for expression via the written word. Your writing opens people's minds and hearts to new possibilities and opportunities. Your stories deliver personal life messages. Specifically, *Naked Hope* reminded me to stop being so stubborn, to allow myself to be loved, to live with passion, and that it's ok to open up my heart. You never know where it might take you."

I exploded into tears because there it was—a legitimately redeeming reason to write romance novels. Her words freed me to continue doing what my heart wanted and what clearly aligned with my soul.

### No longer a closet-writer

Soon after that, I was at dinner with a few friends and heard myself say, "I think I'll write a cowboy romance." I was as surprised to hear myself say that as they were. Their eyes darted back and forth until one of them giggled, and then we all broke out in laughter because what do I know about cowboys? Or horses? Or the rodeo? Or ranching?

Of course, it wasn't my idea at all. My celestial network had whispered it into my ear… and the nudge didn't go away until I began to take it seriously. Suddenly, my contemporary cowboy romance, *Liberty Starr* was born.

Writing *Liberty Starr* was a joyful experience. Every time I sat down to write, I was at the foot of the Rockies riding horses, or bathing in a waterfall and falling in love with a cowboy who wasn't just an ordinary cowboy (my apologies to all you cowboys out there).

Following that, the characters from a poem I'd written two years earlier began to visit me, both in my sleep and while I was awake, and I realized they had more to say. The problem was that they were pilgrims, and no one wants to read a sexy book about pilgrims. Yet, they kept coming to me until I realized I could make the characters anything—they didn't have to be pilgrims—they just wanted their story told. They kept repeating, "wild the wind—wild the wind." So, I wrote *Wild the Wind*—a historical romance with mystical and erotic elements, and it was one wild ride!

With each novel, I have been given the gift of bending time. I don't know how it happens. It just does. What I'm able to get done in the amount of time I spend doing it, is a celestial gift. Then, in February, ten months after I began to write in the women's fiction romance genre, I was offered a publishing contract for the cowboy story. *Liberty Starr* will be released in June 2010 by Carina Press, an imprint of Harlequin.

The day after I was offered my contract with Carina Press, my foot began to feel better. It still likes to tell me that it's not entirely happy with me. I suppose that means I have more work to do—but I am grateful for the relief.

### The Ultimate Ah-ha
Since September of 2005, my friend Joyce and I have celebrated one or both of our birthdays each year by having a joint session with intuitive astrologer Nancy Jernander. This year, my sister joined us. Nancy looked at our charts and said to my sister, "Life isn't always easy for you because when you decided to come back into this world, you signed up for every challenge you could think of. Your attitude was, 'bring it on. I want to get it all resolved'. So at times, the world can be overwhelming to you."

She looked at Joyce and said, your attitude was, 'if I'm going back into the world, I want to cover all my bets and have only the challenges for which I'm best suited'. So you carefully aligned your challenges with your strengths to give you the best odds at overcoming those challenges."

Then she looked at me and began to chuckle. "Rebecca, when you decided to do another life, you said, 'I just want to have fun. I want to make things beautiful and re-introduce romance to the world. I want to be playful and laugh. In this lifetime, I just want to be entertaining, and bring joy to others'."

My judgment kicked in and I said, "Wow, I sound terribly superficial."

Nancy was quick to point out, "Enjoyment is a great challenge to choose. And not an easy one."

Suddenly, I remembered that my guides had shown me that to be truly happy, you have to re-up every day. Wanda's words, "You have a joyous soul," came back to me. I realized how much Ariana came to me as I was wrote my novels—how much I felt her glee and saw the way her laughter embedded itself in my novels. It was the ultimate ah-ha. I've felt so much lighter ever since because I could finally let go of the need to be taken so seriously—a goal that has been a constant source of pressure and focus on enjoyment, and help others do the same. To bring romance to people. To re-introduce love, and the many forms it takes.

No wonder I've wanted to write romances since I was twelve!

I said it before. When we do what we love—what we chose to do before coming into this world—things fall into place—for us—and for others. When we do what we love, we send out a vibration into the world that affects others in a positive way.

Immanuel Kant, an 18th century philosopher defined the rules for happiness as "having someone to love, something to do, and something to hope for." I've adopted Kant's philosophy as my own, and am learning to embrace hope. Some day I intend to be a full time author. I'd like that day to be now. But what I know is that there is such a thing as divine timing. It has to do with our human need to have something hope for.

In today's world where we value the *instantaneousness* of a thing almost more than the thing itself, hope doesn't get a lot of positive press. Hope represents 'waiting' and we don't like to wait. Hope and divine timing allow us to anticipate and desire things we don't have the courage to reach for... until that divine moment we do.

As a romance author, I am beginning to feel comfortable using the voice I worked so hard to find. In 2008 when *Ariana Sings* was released, the last chapter of the book focused on the divineness of being human. Each day, I write about the human body and the heart—how they respond to love, to desire, to joy, to pleasure, to sadness, to hope. Through this adventure, I have come into an important *remembering*—that love is unstoppable, and the human body, divine.

Joyfully,

Rebecca E. Grant

*Love is unstoppable!*

# Reflections

This section is designed to help readers reflect on the key messages from each chapter.

**Beginnings**

- Every human being has a soul. Our souls have a name. As part of my spiritual journey, my soul revealed her name to me. If this is important to you, and you ask from your heart, it will be revealed.

- People are a gift. Many of them come to us when we need them most as 'plain-clothes angels'—unrecognizable, often unassuming, yet their impact is so powerful.

- Depression. If you are experiencing depression, it's important to get professional medical help. In addition to medical help, I found that the Healing Pen Pal Program on Echo Bodine's website was of great benefit. I urge you to contact them by email, even if you are skeptical. I was!

- My spiritual guides and my mother had been trying to reach me for years. Are you listening to your spiritual guides?

- Is there a change coming in your life? What messages might your guides be sending you about the road ahead?

**Change — November 2, 2006**

- How do you respond to change?

- Have you ever experienced depression with yourself or others? If so, how do you deal with it?

- The Healing Pen Pal Program contact information can be found on the Resources page of this book.

- In this chapter I wrote, "If I were to sum up what I've written about thus far in one sentence, I would say that I could not find my voice; that is, I hadn't remembered who I was, and why I chose this lifetime, and this caused me to feel so separate from myself that I experienced erratic bouts of depression." Are you in touch with who you are and why you're currently engaged in a human life?

- When we ask for help, we often find it is already there; frequently in the form of self-empowerment.

**Awakening: Session One out of Six**
- Do you know your spiritual guides? Would you like an introduction?

- The most important message of this book is that the universe is structured around only one thing: endless love. Judgment, inadequacy, failure; none of these things interfere with the love God has for us. Our guides provide wisdom, guidance and love. They do not judge, become angry, or abandon us.

**Discovery**
- Here is the message of love again. We are created in love to love and be loved. When you reflect on this, can you feel it?

- Head vs. heart: the head is analytical. It asks questions but never provides conclusive answers. It is the heart that knows. When we think from our hearts, the truth becomes clear.

- Multiple lives: I am not the expert on this. Both Trish Lapid and Nancy Jernander can tell you more about multiple lifetimes, karma, fulfilling our life's purpose and related matters. More importantly, they can tell you about you! But isn't it wonderful to know that there is no end, and that it all matters. All of it. Always.

- We are all spiritual beings engaged in a human experience. What does this mean to you?

- We are all supported by an abundance of souls; guides, angels, ascended masters, and other specialists; souls who agreed to be supporters in this lifetime. What agreements did you make before coming into this world?

**Unfolding**
- Healing: how are you healed? What requires healing in your life? How do you help others heal?

- We are never alone. Our guides want us to talk to them, to ask, and most importantly, to listen.

## Letting Go: Session Two of Six
- Wonder Woman's shield. How might this be useful?

## Trust: Session Three of Six
- Self-empowerment is amazingly freeing. Are there places where self-empowerment might be useful to you?

- The tool of entrainment. Do you know what it is? Can you think of opportunities to employ this tool?

- What happens when we have learned one of our life's lessons well, but don't realize it?

## Balance: Session four of six
- Reframing how we think of something is helpful. When we open up to someone or something, the very act of opening up changes the energy and thus the reality of the moment. We begin to create our own reality; the reality we desire

- Using the shield and the bamboo bowl. How might that be useful?

- Emotional intelligence: where are you in terms of your emotional intelligence. Why is this important?

- Healing: we are all healers. What is one of the most common (and important) ways we heal others?

## Unity: December 6, 2006
- When I was domed by golden light, I felt both present in human form, but also saw myself floating above the table where I joined with another soul. Have you ever felt an experience like this, in whole or in part? What was going on at the time?

## Wet Death: Session Five of Six
- Sometimes we have to let go of what doesn't serve us well anymore so that we can more fully integrate with our soul (or higher consciousness).

- I have found the image of my guides circling around me in clockwise motion while they called in healers, to be very comforting. When I visualize this, I can see my light growing brighter. This may be a helpful image for you.

- We all break, we are all healable, and sometimes our light grows brighter because of the learning that produces our tears.

**Peace: Session Six of Six**
- Soul Visit: this is a process that has been extremely helpful to me. I recommend it highly.

- Throw wide the reins: this is a constant reminder that the more we try to control something, the less control we actually have.

- It's time to think from our hearts. The head requires proof; the heart simply knows.

- Nelson Mandela's 'Unite' story. This is the 'meet them where they are at and take them up one level at a time' method. It might be helpful to begin by asking (silently) 'at what level do we need to travel?' This is the art of entrainment. Entrainment is one component of emotional intelligence.

**Gathering**
- Are you feeling stuck? Is there something you'd like to do? Remember Lawrence Raab's poem, *My Life Before I Knew It*? By doing something, *anything* creatively, it will shift your energy and may lead you to what you really want to do.

- I want to love myself into being: this is a phrase worth meditating about. This is about the love of self and the desire for wholeness.

- "If you ask us we will answer"—This is the everlasting message from our guides. Ask them!

- Basic physics – the law of attraction: we attract to us what we are most focused on. I was focused on the disbelief that I was truly writing again. Because of this, I literally caused myself to be unable to write. What are you focusing on?

### Flying Lessons:  June, 2007
- Spiritual connectedness to nature and animal totems. This may or may not resonate with you. Why or why not?

### Rhythm:  August, 2007
- There is no judgment – everything is love.

- Remember to ask from the heart

- We are never alone! Animal totem website can be found in the resources section of this book.

- The rhythm of life. Have you given away pieces of your soul?  Call them back and begin healing!

### Ariana Sings:  August, 2007
- Learning the name of my soul gave me greater ability to access my higher consciousness; but the real gift was that because I asked from my heart, I was given the answer.

### Bending Time — August – September, 2007
- Balancing ego with human spirituality. How much do you love yourself?

- Can you embrace your imperfections as part of the human experience?

- The model for spiritual connectedness and fulfillment helps us understand the way in which our human components and our spiritual components are interconnected and integrated and demonstrates how separateness, which is the source of all pain (fear, conflict, anger) is an illusion suggested by ego.

### Harmony:  October, 2007
- If you are asked, pass it on!  This is a form of 'paying it forward'.

### One Love:  December, 2007
- Learning to listen with soft ears means to listen in a new way so that we hear truth rather than mere words. It is a complement to looking at the world through soft eyes without judgment.

- Take your gifts into the world  sooner rather than later!  Don't delay!

- If you keep forgetting something, the same something, it may very likely be a message from your guides – ask, then listen.

- We are spiritual beings engaged in a human experience. What does this mean to you?

- Being in body is as important as living out of body in the ether. It is all about love. How we contribute to love is different depending on who we are, regardless of whether we're in body or in the ether. Experience the love. Be the bowl.

# Resources

Trish Lapid Manning
Development Coach
Certified Energetic Practitioner
trish.manning@pagasalifework.com
www.pagasalifework.com

Nancy Jernander
Intuitive astrologer
Also be found on Echo Bodine's 'resources' page:
http://www.echobodine.com/refer.htm
idostargazing@yahoo.com

Phyllis Smith
Fiber Artist and Seamstress / Tailor
Soul quilts, story quilts, memory quilts
email: phyllissmith@earthlink.net
www.river-isle.com
www.alterationsbyphyllis.com

Kricket Opheim
Minnesota Licensed Realtor
Email: Kricket@cbburnet.com
Website: www.kricketandmike.com

Tracy Griffin, Artist
GriffinArtStudios.com
tracy.griffin@hotmail.com

Lena Swanson
Animal Communication
Email: eswanson@ties2.net
Website: www.lenaswanson.com

Healing Pen Pal Program
http://www.echobodine.com/penpals.htm

Dr. Marcie New
Doctor of Chiropractic
612-866-3083

## Published Works Cited

Chardin, Pierre Teilhard, revised English translation by Benjamin Wall (1975), *The Phenomenon of Man*, New York, HarperCollins.

Pearsall, Paul, (1998); *The Heart's Code; Tapping the Wisdom and Power of our Heart Energy*; Broadway Books; New York, NY.

Hall, Meredith, *Outport Shadows*; Prairie Schooner, Volume 80, Number 1, Spring 2006, pp. 48-59.

## Artwork

Cover Art: Watercolor: *Evening Sea Cliffs* by artist Tracy Griffin
GriffinArtStudios.com
tracy.griffin@hotmail.com


*Amaranthine Love Acknowledged* by artist Phyllis Smith
www.river-isle.com
www.alterationsbyphyllis.com
www.etsy.com/shop/dancingfabrics
phyllissmith@earthlink.net
or look for 'Dancing Fabrics' on Facebook and flickr

## Acknowledgments

My deepest appreciation and gratitude to Elizabeth, Joyce, Nancy, Trish, Phyllis, Linda, Thomas, and Lee without whom this story could not be told.

## About the Author

**Rebecca E. Grant** believes that love is *unstoppable!* Currently an innovative educator with a PhD in organizational development, Rebecca lives on the edge of a wetlands in Minnesota where wild turkeys and other creatures provide balance and renewal. She loves the four seasons, long walks, early morning with a steaming cup of coffee, and late nights filled with stimulating conversation, a bottle of amusingly insouciant wine, and good friends.

Rebecca writes creative nonfiction, women's fiction and romance, poetry, and children's books.

Find her at:

www.RebeccaEGrant.com

blog.RebeccaEGrant.com

Rebecca@RebeccaEGrant.com